The Ethnic Southerners

Other Books by George Brown Tindall

South Carolina Negroes, 1877–1900

The Emergence of the New South, 1913–1945

The Disruption of the Solid South

The Persistent Tradition in New South Politics

The Pursuit of Southern History:
Presidential Addresses of the Southern
Historical Association, 1935–1963 (editor)

A Populist Reader (editor)

GEORGE BROWN TINDALL

The

Ethnic

Southerners

SIANA STATE UNIVERSITY PRESS

BATON ROUGE

Designer: Albert Crochet
Typeface: VIP Baskerville
Typesetter: G & S Typesetters
1977 printing

LIBRARY OF CONGRESS CATALOGING IN PUBLICATION DATA
Tindall, George Brown.
    The ethnic Southerners.

    Includes index.
    1. Southern States—Civilization—Addresses, essays,
lectures. I. Title.
F209.T54   309.1'75'04   76-40474
ISBN 0-8071-0258-X

To three teachers

J. Mauldin Lesesne
Delbert H. Gilpatrick
Meta E. Gilpatrick

Contents

Preface

As long ago as 1869 John William De Forest, a union officer reporting on the postbellum South Carolinians, was telling the readers of *Harper's New Monthly Magazine*, "We shall do well to study this peculiar people, which will soon lose its peculiarities." De Forest was neither the first nor the last of his tribe. South-watchers before and since have been haunted by the premonition that regional peculiarities were forever being engulfed in the crosscurrents of change.

In these latter days there is still no end of elegists bidding farewell to the South and announcing the Americanization of Dixie. Gradually the suspicion grows that the everlasting farewells only bear witness to the enduring spell cast by the South. The obituarians have been at it so long, in fact, as to become themselves a venerable tradition of the region. And if they keep it up much longer, their Vanishing South will have staged one of the most prolonged disappearing acts since the decline and fall of Rome.

What De Forest and his successors have been watching, perhaps, is less a disappearing act than a transformation scene. In two centuries of American independence the South, like Proteus, has assumed many

ix

shapes in the hands of those who wrestle with its identity. The image of the Tidewater aristocrats yielded in
turn to images of Jacksonian frontiersmen, chivalrous
Southrons, proslavery firebrands, embattled Rebels, New
South boosters, insurgent Populists, and a twentieth-
century mosaic of patricians, rednecks, village nabobs,
and good old boys—among others. Images of southern
ladies and southern blacks have gone through similar
mutations.

Even the hypothetical borders of Dixie are mutable.
Few would challenge the title-deed of the eleven erst-
while Confederate states, even though Texas and Florida run out into mesquite country and mangrove
swamps. It is common to annex Kentucky and Oklahoma to form a thirteen-state region, and it was once
the practice to add those other parts where slavery en-
dured longest: Missouri, West Virginia, Maryland, Delaware, and the District of Columbia. All of these but
Missouri still make up the "Census South," and all but
the District of Columbia are represented in the Southern Governors' Conference, along with Puerto Rico and
the Virgin Islands.

The variations abound. Howard W. Odum, after he
had appraised nearly seven hundred indices from the
1930 census, identified two southern regions: a Southeast which extended to Kentucky, and a Southwest
which linked Texas and Oklahoma with New Mexico
and Arizona. Now the latest seers are putting them back
together again. After the thirty turbulent years which
Charles P. Roland calls the South's "improbable era,"
they have sighted on the southern horizons an extended
"Sunbelt" reaching from coast to coast, its economy
battening on "agribusiness," defense, technology, oil,

real estate, tourism, and leisure. The migratory Americans, they note, have begun to follow the sun in search of prosperity, retirement havens, and general jollification. Reincarnated as the imperial Sunbelt, the region is about to assume a new role—or resume a forgotten role —as arbiter of the national destiny.

All this, of course, will have to meet the test of time. It may be that the gurus of the Sunbelt have sighted a mirage lifted by overheated growth along the Gulf Crescent and in the southwestern deserts—or by their own fevered imaginations. But whatever the future may hold, the South has repeatedly displayed a striking knack for accepting change without losing the sense of its separate identity. In the 1920s it was the consciousness of change that gave to the Southern Renaissance in literature its special flavor and to fundamentalism and Ku Kluxry their peculiar virulence. The same consciousness inspired the regional self-discovery of the 1930s, reflected in agrarianism, regionalism, the vivid documentary literature of the period, and the rising protest against the "colonial economy."

For some years afterward the awareness of regional distinctiveness faded. Even the South came under the sway of what historian John Higham called the consensus school, governed by the supposition that social and economic change would quickly obliterate both the ethnic and the regional differences in American life. But since the mid-1960s, as Higham has noted more recently, historians and social scientists have engaged in "a repudiation of consensus and an invocation of community." Instead of extolling homogeneity, they have begun to take notice of persistent ethnic groups, "divergent unities," "unstable pluralism," an "unsettled people," a "segmented society." In doing so, they express what has become a popular as well as a scholarly perception.

The renewed attention to differences in American life suggests a reexamination of some neglected celebrations of diversity: Frederick Jackson Turner's observation that the United States had become a congeries of sections and that "the sections serve as restraints upon a deadly uniformity," or Josiah Royce's invocation of provincial loyalty as a means toward *"educating the self-estranged spirit of our nation to know itself better,"* much as the Englishman's ties to his native heath or the Austrian's devotion to his *heimat* paradoxically bolstered national loyalties. Such views suffused the broad concept of regionalism which southerners like Howard Odum and Rupert Vance elaborated in the 1930s.

More recently Nathan Glazer and Daniel P. Moynihan, in revising their study of persistent ethnicity, suggested that assimilation was "inhibited by the unavailability of a simple 'American' identity. One is a New Englander, or a Southerner, or a Midwesterner, and all these things mean something too concrete for the ethnic to adopt completely, while excluding his ethnic identity." The pursuit of regional history, therefore, need not be, and in its most vigorous areas is not, an exercise in antiquarianism—or in sectional defensiveness.

To note that southern history remains relevant to live issues, however, is not to plump for a presentist approach to history. Knowing things for the sake of knowledge itself is not an unworthy goal, and one can never foresee what kinds of relevance may emerge. Merely to mention the salient themes in the southern transformation of our own times is to bear out the point. The second Reconstruction of recent years had manifest parallels in the first, and deep roots there, especially in the Reconstruction amendments. Even the study of slavery, a subject that once seemed to be depleted, has assumed new urgency in the light of our own times.

The processes of economic change may be less dramatic, but they are at least as important, if badly neglected. The transition from farming to "agribusiness," industrial growth, corporate and labor history, the story of state and community promotional efforts, of the painful processes by which the South has been emerging from poverty to affluence—these have relation both to the present South and to an underdeveloped world. The New South's devotion to economic growth weathered the assumptions of the 1930s that the frontiers of a mature economy were exhausted; and there is reason to believe that, for better or for worse, the growth psychology will weather the zero-growth philosophies of the 1970s.

In politics the gradual unfolding of a two-party system has given new pertinence to the party struggles of those lost years before the triumph of Jim Crow and the Solid South at the turn of the century, to the long-frustrated efforts to revive southern Republicanism, and to the tangled question of black disfranchisement: Who engineered it and who profited most from it?

The following essays were prepared for various occasions and purposes during the South's "improbable era," and all were more or less influenced by an awareness that change had become the southern way of life. The earliest was first published in 1958 and the most recent in 1975. The first five address themselves mainly to the persistence and transformation of the regional identity. The others deal chiefly with aspects of change in racial practices, politics, and economics, and their historical roots and parallels. Much of the substance from three of the essays was incorporated in *The Emergence of the New South, 1913–1945*: "The Benighted South," "Business Progressivism," and "The 'Colonial Economy.'" After some hesitation they were included because they highlight points that were less salient in the larger volume. "The Southern Strategy" summarizes the main arguments that are developed in more detail in *The Disruption of the Solid South*.

GEORGE B. TINDALL

Chapel Hill
March, 1976

Acknowledgments

I AM GRATEFUL TO PETER H. WOOD FOR ENCOURAGING ME to pursue the parallels between ethnicity and regional identity and to Beverly Jarrett for editorial assistance and invincible patience which has now survived three manuscripts.

The essays in this volume are reprinted from the several publications in which they first appeared. They have been revised slightly with an eye to style and to the elimination of topical references, repetitions, and anachronisms, some of which proved inescapable, but without alteration of substantive content. Footnotes which originally accompanied some of the essays have been omitted here.

For permission to reprint the essays I am grateful to the original publishers, as shown below:

"Beyond the Mainstream: The Ethnic Southerners," *Journal of Southern History*, XL (January, 1974), 3–18. Copyright 1974 by the Southern Historical Association. Reprinted by permission of the Managing Editor. Delivered as a presidential address to the Southern Historical Association, Atlanta, 1973.

"Mythology: A New Frontier in Southern History," in Frank E. Vandiver (ed.), *The Idea of the South: Pursuit of a Central Theme* (Chicago: University of Chicago Press, 1964), 1–15. Delivered to a semicentennial symposium at Rice University, 1963, and published with other papers in the same series.

"The Benighted South: Origins of a Modern Image," *Virginia Quarterly Review*, XL (Spring, 1964), 281–94. Delivered to a session of the American Historical Association, Philadelphia, 1963.

"The Central Theme Revisited," in Charles G. Sellers, Jr. (ed.), *The Southerner as American* (Chapel Hill: University of North Carolina Press, 1960), 104–29. Delivered in an earlier version to a session of the American Historical Association, Washington, 1955.

"The Significance of Howard W. Odum to Southern History: A Preliminary Estimate," *Journal of Southern History*, XXIV (August, 1958), 285–307. Copyright 1958 by the Southern Historical Association. Reprinted by permission of the Managing Editor. Delivered to a session of the Southern Sociological Society, Asheville, 1958. Reprinted here under a shorter title.

"The Southern Strategy: A Historical Perspective," *North Carolina Historical Review*, XLVIII (Spring, 1971), 126–41. Delivered to a session of the Literary and Historical Association of North Carolina, Greensboro, 1971.

"Business Progressivism: Southern Politics in the Twenties," *South Atlantic Quarterly*, LXII (Winter, 1963), 92–106; copyright Duke University Press. Delivered to a seminar at Johns Hopkins University, 1962.

"Populism: A Semantic Identity Crisis," *Virginia Quarterly Review*, XLVIII (Autumn, 1972), 501–18. Delivered as the Rembert W. Patrick Memorial Lecture at Guilford College, 1972.

"The Bubble in the Sun," *American Heritage*, XVI (August, 1965), 76–83, 109–11. Reprinted in *Great Stories of American Businessmen* (New York: American Heritage Publishing Company, 1972). Copyright 1965 by American Heritage Publishing Co., Inc. Reprinted by permission from American Heritage.

"The 'Colonial Economy' and the Growth Psychology: The South in the 1930s," *South Atlantic Quarterly*, LXIV (Autumn, 1965), 465–77; copyright Duke University Press. Delivered to a symposium on "The Impact of Education, Science, and Technology on the South" at Duke University, 1965.

"Onward and Upward with the Rising South," in Donald R. Noble and Joab L. Thomas (eds.), *The Rising South*, Volume I, *Changes and Issues* (University, Ala.: University of Alabama Press, 1976), 10–24. Delivered to a symposium on "The Rising South" at the University of Alabama, Tuscaloosa, 1974, and in an altered version to the Harnett County Forum, Campbell College, 1975. First published in *Harnett County Forum, 1975*.

The Ethnic Southerners

1

Beyond the Mainstream:
The Ethnic Southerners

A FEW YEARS AGO A NEWSMAN BASED IN ATLANTA SENT forth to the readers of *Esquire* the good news that "the South is over" and then proceeded to elaborate "some of the ways the cracker crumbled." His findings were hardly without precedent, although expressed with more wit than we have come to expect in such write-ups. The Vanishing South has long been staple fare at regional symposia—just as surely as the rubber chicken and petrified peas. Looking back to the late 1950s, we can find Harry S. Ashmore carving out an epitaph for Dixie, and John T. Westbrook heralding "the happy truth that the South . . . [had] lost its 'regional integrity'" and grown "rich . . . urban, industrialized, and no longer 'Southern,' but rather northernized, Europeanized, cosmopolitan." Ten years before Ashmore and Westbrook, Charles S. Johnson published a study of changing race relations which he called *Into the Main Stream*. For a generation now the metaphor has been so often applied to the South, black and white, and so often repeated that there has been little reason to doubt the conventional wisdom that the benighted South was beginning to see the light, that it was getting right with God and was gathering down by the mainstream of American life for baptism by total immersion.

The belief that the South is forever disappearing has a long and honored tradition. It has affected southerners of every walk and every faith, including those who resisted the thought that the distinctive region might become one with Nineveh and Tyre. The New South creed of the nineteenth century, according to Paul M. Gaston, promised to make the South, like the nation, "rich, triumphant, and morally innocent." New South liberals looked forward to a region absorbed into the national abundance of both progress and equality. Assimilation seemed most of all the goal of black southerners, who became in many ways the most nationalistic of all Americans. Even after repeated betrayals, their faith in the nation, in its promise and its Constitution, continued to flicker and sometimes to flame.

But the white South, too, had a claim on nationalism. In the beginning a white southerner had defined the American Creed. Much later, the prophets of a New South looked upon the sectional conflict as the great aberration; they sought the true South in the world of the founding fathers and once again embraced the national myths. In the Spanish-American War, and more intensely in the First World War, the South went through its own peculiar "Americanization" in the melting pot of patriotism. The idea that the South embodied the purest Americanism (with overtones of nativism and fundamentalism) grew into an established article of the regional faith. And during the years of the New Deal and the Second World War, the South entered still more fully into the orbit of national affairs.

By the 1950s and 1960s southern distinctiveness appeared to be doomed. In quick sequence the region encountered the bulldozer revolution, the urban breakthrough, the civil rights movement, the black revolt, and the disruption of the Solid South. Socioeconomic change fast eroded old landmarks, and sociologists took to listing the indices of a Vanishing South as eagerly as they had once enumerated the indices of a deficient South. In a presidential address to the Southern Sociological Society Selz C. Mayo chose to speak in 1964 on the "Disappearing Sectional South" and quoted George L. Simpson on the facts of change: "the movement from rural to urban; from one crop to diversification . . . from bad health to good health; from about one-half the national per capita income to nearly three-fourths; from some 1,280,000 to nearly 2,500,000 industrial workers; from the kerosene lamp to universal electricity and the winking eye of television; from one world of race relations to another." In 1971, in the *American Sociological Review*, John C. McKinney and Linda Brookover Bourque discounted as illusory the "southern mystique," "the belletristic tradition [of] . . . local color," and the mass media's fascination with southern idiosyncrasy. They dwelt instead on solid evidence that confirmed an "increasing similarity between the South and non-South" in the realms of urbanization, industry, occupations, income, and education.

Yet since the mid-1960s the existence, certainly the appearance, of consensus in American life has been visibly shaken. The suspicion grows that the legend of a homogenized American culture had all along the shimmering quality of mirage, like those situation comedies where people live in boxes made of ticky-tacky and all look the same. It is not the South that has vanished but the mainstream, like one of those desert rivers that run out into the sand, consumed by the heat.

The convulsions of recent years have made manifest what David M. Potter called "the unseen revolution of the 1920's and 1930's." In a posthumous essay published in 1973, Potter suggested that conformity rather than compulsion had long provided the chief sanction against disruption in American life and that this meant conformity mainly to the values of a dominant white Anglo-Saxon Protestant culture. By the 1920s and 1930s, however, those values had suffered crippling blows, most conspicuously in the failure of prohibition and the social trauma of the Great Depression. Perhaps most crippling of all had been the rise of a new class, the academic intellectuals who "set busily about laying their axes to the mythic underpinnings of the American identity."

By the 1960s, therefore, defenders of the society had become guiltily aware of its failure to fulfill its own promises and "disarmed also by their broad, absolutist, and somewhat indiscriminate ideas of the right to dissent." The almost simultaneous disintegration of the civil rights movement and of the Vietnam situation gave rise to a major crisis of confidence. A severe case of war weariness—involving wars foreign and domestic—seized the nation. Amid the tumult, the mass media, often thought to be agents for conformity, fostered counterforces instead: black revolt, student rebellion, fem lib, food fads, hard rock, the cult of slovenliness, raw incivility and violence, pornography, and the occult—and the more bizarre the better.

Then came the backlash. Its source was said to be the silent majority, the Middle American. "There is hardly a language to describe him," Peter Schrag wrote in *Harper's*, "or even a set of social statistics. Just names: racist-bigot-redneck-ethnic-Irish-Italian-Pole-Hunkie-Yahoo. The lower middle class. A blank. The man under whose hat lies the great American desert. Who watches the tube, plays the horses, and keeps the niggers out of his union and his neighborhood. Who might vote for Wallace (but didn't). Who cheers when the cops beat up on demonstrators. Who is free, white, and twenty-one, has a job, a home, a family, and is up to his eyeballs in credit. In the guise of the working class . . . he was once the hero of the civics book. . . . Now he is 'the forgotten man,' perhaps the most alienated person in America." The description, it should be noted, was ironic, a parody of the respectable bigotry that had infected a fashionable elite.

In the strange new world of the 1960s history manifested some further ironies. The "most alienated person" was the one who flew the flag and invented a new symbol of loyalty, the hard hat. To be a worker or a *petit bourgeois* was no longer to command the respect of the media. What was in some ways a display of class consciousness, therefore, turned into a display of ethnic identity, for it was among the workers and lower middle class that large, perhaps the largest, portions of second- and third-generation immigrant stock had found lodgment. And their behavior followed in spirit, if not in mathematical fidelity, Marcus Lee Hansen's law that the second generation embraced Americanism and the third generation rediscovered its heritage. Something like this had happened in the progression from civil rights and Americanism to black power and the Afro-American identity. Now the new ethnicity manifested striking parallels. Indeed, it conferred on black power the sincerest form of flattery, imitation.

Few hints of its coming appeared in the writings of either historians or sociologists. In the 1950s the writings of both belonged mainly to the consensus school. Then in the early 1960s three studies adduced significant evidence of enduring diversity in American society and culture. In Gerhard E. Lenski's *The Religious Factor* and in Nathan Glazer and Daniel P. Moynihan's *Beyond the Melting Pot*, social studies of Detroit and New York respectively, it appeared that ethnic and religious factors continued to account for many personal attitudes toward matters social, cultural, and political. In a broader study, Milton M. Gordon's *Assimilation in American Life*, it appeared that pluralism rather than uniformity represented the "overwhelming reality" of American culture.

These studies were but harbingers of a broadening interest in ethnic identity, at first among social scientists and now in the public press. All of a sudden pop writings upstaged scholarship, and the new ethnicity became the latest bandwagon. We find it in books like Peter Schrag's *The Decline of the WASP*, Andrew M. Greeley's *Why Can't They Be Like Us?*, and Michael Novak's *The Rise of the Unmeltable Ethnics*, which pronounces the 1970s the "Decade of the Ethnics" and celebrates a group Novak perversely calls the PIGS, which is an acronym for Poles, Italians, Greeks, and Slavs. The theme crops up in the papers, in the magazines, and in films like *The Godfather*. Foundations have staged symposia on the subject, they are sponsoring more ethnic studies, and one journal (issued from Nashville) has printed a special issue on the rediscovery of ethnicity. Lapel buttons read "Kiss me—I'm Czech [or whatever]." And at least one drugstore now uses "Ethnic Needs" as a euphemism for Negro cosmetics.

The first reaction of a southerner to all this is apt to be that it has little to do with him. It may be true that back in 1809 David Ramsay could write in his *History of South Carolina*: "So many and so various have been the sources from which Carolina has derived her population, that a considerable period must elapse, before the people amalgamate into a mass possessing an uniform national character." But a considerable period *has* elapsed. Perhaps, to be sure, there are still those exceptions which prove the rule: a few reminders of forgotten Spaniards and Frenchmen, some Mexican-Americans renamed Chicanos, some Cuban cigar-makers and the more recent Cuban refugees, some German counties out in Texas, Cajuns up the bayous, Italians in New Orleans, Hungarians over in Tangipahoa Parish, a scattering of Czechs, Dutch, Ukranians, and in Mississippi, even Chinese. Jews are visible, if scarce, in most localities; politicians in Charleston used to reckon with the Irish and Germans; and there are those enclaves of mixed-blood Lumbees, Tuscaroras, "Brass Ankles," Melungeons, and Turks, not to mention remnants of Cherokees, Catawbas, Creeks, and Seminoles. One might even have to throw in those quaint hillbillies, who have achieved ethnic identity as "Yesterday's People"

by strumming dulcimers and singing Elizabethan bal-
lads when not employed in shooting their neighbors or
distilling forty-rod bug juice back in the coves.

And if, out in the boondocks of the North, hillbilly has
become a synonym for southerner, the perception may
be more acute than one might think. For the South *is*
the habitat of the quintessential WASP. Is it not, in fact,
the biggest single WASP nest this side of the Atlantic? Is
it not, perhaps, the one part of the country where the
melting pot really worked, because so few ingredients
were added after independence? Over the years all
those southerners with names like Kruttschnitt, Kolb,
DeBardeleben, Huger, Lanneau, Toledano, Moise,
Jastremski, or Cheros got melted down and poured
back out in the mold of good old boys and girls, if not of
the gentry. Who, for example, could be more WASPish
than Scarlett O'Hara, in more ways than one?

At the same time, and too often forgotten, a separate
and unequal melting pot bubbled away all the more
furiously. Is there not "a sense," Michael G. Kammen
has asked, "in which the melting pot notion is more
applicable within the black American nation than within
the white? There was great diversity in the African
origins of American Negroes: regional, linguistic, and
tribal differences, as well as in their prior condition of
freedom. . . . Despite this diversity, however, Africans
were forcibly homogenized after several generations
into a fairly singular Afro-American mold with common
folkways. Thus, the only American melting pot has perhaps been a black one, though in this case the putative
pot has been reluctant to call the kettle black."

However surprising it may sound at first, the function
of melting pots is to create new ethnic groups. Every-

body has a melting pot in his past, and two of them have been located down home, with some of the same ingredients going into both. The two ethnic groups, black and white, which have emerged from the crucibles of the South, have been reluctant to acknowledge kinship, but each has been keenly aware of its separate identity in the nation.

The North, that "significant other," has been equally aware, most acutely when southerners move into the hillbilly or black ghettos of Chicago or New York—or conversely, when Yankees populate Houston or Huntsville. Flannery O'Connor once told of a friend from Wisconsin who came to Atlanta and bought a house in the suburbs. The man who sold it was from Massachusetts and recommended the property by saying: "'You'll like this neighborhood. There's not a Southerner for two miles.' At least," Miss O'Connor added, "we can be identified when we do occur."

For more than a century the South has been a seedbed of population and cultural styles for the rest of the country. We have progressed (or receded) from things like minstrel shows, cavalier romances, and bourbon whiskey to things like Coca-Cola, *Gone with the Wind*, and the latter-day Ku Klux Klan, each of which was first bottled in Atlanta. Southern styles have threatened to conquer the fields of writing and pop culture. Blacks exported spirituals, jazz, blues, slang, and southern cuisine in the guise of "soul food." The good old boys finally arrived with "countrypolitan" music, bluegrass, and stock-car racing. One of those stock-car racers was Junior Johnson, who learned the trade running his daddy's moonshine out of Ingle Hollow. And in one of Tom (not Thomas) Wolfe's hopped-up essays Johnson was anointed the "Last American Hero." But at the time, like most of us, Wolfe overlooked the potential of an old country lawyer named Samuel James Ervin, Jr., who lived just down the mountains a piece and still harbored a quaint faith in the Bill of Rights.

At times the South appears to have a premonitory sense of coming styles. For instance, two salient styles of the 1960s, public demonstrations and the generation gap, arrived simultaneously with the student sit-ins at Greensboro, which started one month after the decade began. The lazy South cultivated the art of relaxation long before the greening of America and the fashion of "overhauls" long before the jeaning of America. When the cult of outward poverty became the in-thing, the profits accrued to southern textile and garment mills, not to mention the few cotton farmers who are still around. The makers even learned to fade, fray, and patch the fabric in advance, thus sparing consumers the trouble of what southerners once had to do for themselves. Now the youth cult has discovered Pentecost and gospel songs. Other rebels, preaching participatory democracy, have joined the attack on Leviathan which southerners kept up throughout the whole descent from Williamsburg to Watergate.

Some educational work remains to be done, however. Only a tin ear, or an unaccountable deafness to regional intonations, can explain the current fashion of omitting the "r" when spelling "Miz." Anybody who had been properly raised would know better than that. Perhaps the northern culture lag can be fully corrected only when the South can export some real educators like Al Capp's fictional Earthquake McGoon, who was rescued from a lynch mob in Dogpatch so that he might accept tenure as the first professor of redneck studies at Harvard University, where he introduced the elite to the fundamentals of hillbilly logic.

The average inhabitant of the non-South, however, has trouble getting the hang of it. Like members of other tribes, he is apt to resist the intrusion of exotic cultures and apt to view them as hostile and threatening. One septentrional professor explains, for example, that "high homicide rates in the United States today are related primarily to the persistence of Southern cultural traditions developed before the Civil War and subsequently spreading over much of the country." Another notes that the South "is a distillation of those traits which are the worst (and a few which are the best) in the national character. . . . And the nation reacts emotionally to the South precisely because it subconsciously recognizes itself there." Nor has the South been blameless in the search for scapegoats (New England slave-traders, for instance) or for the great alibi (the Civil War). At the same time southerners, black and white, have made each other into scapegoats and alibis. Both have done the same with immigrant groups of the motley North— and have seen the practice reciprocated.

In the polemics of the new ethnicity, Yankeefied images of the South persist, and there is little recognition of kinship on either side. Yet, Jonathan Daniels wrote years ago, "For good or for ill, being a Southerner is like being a Jew. And, indeed, more needs to be written about the similarity of the minds and the emotions of the Jew, the Irishman, the Southerner, and, perhaps, the Pole, as a basis for the better understanding of each of them and of them all." Their common experience has been migration from a peasant background into the

mills and towns. It has been to bear a common stigma
as the perpetual outsiders, yet for that reason to be
fascinating to other folk. In recent years southerners
(white southerners, at least), like other ethnic groups,
have rallied to the flag—somehow the Stars and Stripes
quickly replaced the Stars and Bars as a symbol of re-
sentment and defiance. And southerners betray a human tenacity in clinging to their heritage. Still, as William Appleman Williams has said, "The visceral essay
on the white southerner as a second-class citizen has yet
to be written. C. Vann Woodward is just too damn
polite. And Norman Mailer has not considered it important enough."

Southern historians all more or less share the rustic
urbanity of Woodward, and lack the urban vulgarity of
Mailer, but whether they chronicle the Vanishing South
or the southerner as American, they all share that in-
stinct Hansen ascribed to the third generation: the need
for roots, for a usable past. They are not given to speaking or writing about ethnic identity, but they have somehow felt the regional differences in their bones. Some
would call this feeling "impressionistic." David Potter, I
think, more aptly spoke of "an awareness of the historical process." But the awareness is overpowered by the
ready assumption that socioeconomic change will quickly erase the differences, although the South has gone
through nearly four centuries of change without disappearing.

Sociologists have reinforced such attitudes both the-
oretically and empirically. They have written copiously
about the transition from folk community to moderniza-
tion or from what Howard Odum called "folkways" to
"stateways" and "technicways," or from what classical

sociology called *Gemeinschaft* to *Gesellschaft*. Sociologists further reinforced the idea by their methods. They focused on those things which could be enumerated, and those were the very things which registered the most visible changes: population, industry, occupations, income, and schooling.

In the last few years, however, some sociologists have turned their attention toward a different kind of data, the opinion polls. As a result, computers have begun to print out quantitative findings which support the "impressionistic" sense of things, and scattered reports on persisting regional differences have begun to surface in the journals. A belief in cultural convergence, to quote one article, seems "based upon little more than the belief that common influences *should* produce greater uniformity." Another piece reports that "in general, Negro-white differences are smaller than the differences between Southern and non-Southern whites. . . . In other words . . . the population of the United States is apparently somewhat more [culturally] divided along regional than along racial lines." If the country is divided into two societies, therefore, as the Kerner Commission asserted, could the two societies be North and South rather than black and white?

The findings so far rest on limited evidence. The reports focus mainly on whites, and all rely on surveys conducted for other purposes, but they have now been summarized and extended in two useful books. Lewis M. Killian, whose perceptions had been heightened by an earlier study of hillbillies in Chicago, recently brought out a book entitled *White Southerners*, which appeared in a series devoted to American ethnic groups. More recently John Shelton Reed published *The Endur-*

ing South: Subcultural Persistence in Mass Society. Both
books demonstrate by their vigorous prose that the
English language remains in style with sociologists despite rumors to the contrary. Both are relatively short
and will repay the time spent with them, although I
propose here to focus on the findings of John Reed.

In *The Enduring South*, Reed asserts "that regional
cultural differences have existed and still exist, and that
they correspond at least roughly to Americans' perceptions of them. These differences are substantial, and
larger than most differences which are thought to be
important in the United States." Using opinion polls
Reed systematically investigates three broad cultural
areas: attitudes toward religion, violence, and localism.
He finds that "Southerners . . . are more likely than
non-Southerners to be conventionally religious, to accept the private use of force (or the potential for it),
and to be anchored in their homeplace." Little of the
difference seems to result from differences in urbanization, occupation, or education. And, surprisingly, the
differences have not decreased in recent years; in some
cases they have actually increased.

In a concluding chapter Reed seeks to explain the
sources of continued distinctiveness. Two institutions,
the family and the church, are found to be more important in the South than in other regions. Two other institutions, the schools and the mass media, appear to be
less influential; both are staffed by southerners who
affect the tone and content of the messages transmitted,
and both impart information to southerners who are
conditioned to receive some messages better than
others. In seeking the ultimate explanation Reed follows
the reasoning of Sheldon Hackney: "Localism, violence,

and a conservative religion are all plausible responses for a minority group, surrounded by a culture which is viewed as powerful, hostile, and unresponsive; all can be seen as adaptive reactions to the situation in which Southerners have, time and again, found themselves." Throughout the book Reed consistently pursues an ethnic analogy. "Southerners' differences from the American mainstream," he writes, "have been similar in kind, if not degree, to those of the immigrant ethnic groups."

There are some lessons for historians in these findings. One of the first is that we have been so caught up in deriving lessons from history and in searching for a usable past that we have neglected the living past of the community. The lessons that southerners in the large have derived from their history—or rather from their communal heritage—are not, properly speaking, lessons at all so much as formative influences which have shaped their identity. The current signposts, therefore, would seem to be pointing southern historians toward those areas in which their contributions have been least developed—the cultural and social history of the region, the study of the South as an American subculture.

In a recent article on "C. Vann Woodward and the Burden of Southern Liberalism," Michael O'Brien has indicated one of the many gaps. "If the South is a habit of thought," O'Brien suggests, "it would follow that Southern history is pre-eminently the history of the Southern mind. But if one looks at the groaning shelves of books on the South, one finds thousands of volumes on its politics, hundreds on its economics and its sociology. . . . There are a few books on the antebellum mind, one or two good things on the New South creed and a reasonable batch of studies on the literary scene since the First World War, but no more. It seems odd, but the answer is simple enough. Southerners have not written their intellectual history because they have not thought the South defined by its mind. The South was a matter of race or politics or economics but not the pattern of its thought."

There are, of course, already some new stirrings in the field of intellectual history; studies of southern intellectuals, academic and otherwise, are recently completed or on the way, and more attention is being given to the mythology which has done so much to shape the sense of southern identity. In the preface to *American Counterpoint*, C. Vann Woodward has pointed out another inviting frontier, the "need for a history of North-South images and stereotypes, of when and how and why they were developed, the shape they took, the uses that have been made of them and how they have been employed from time to time in regional defense, self-flattery, and polemics."

Intellectual history, most broadly conceived, becomes the history of a culture and of the community in which it is rooted. The study of literature and of the people's arts and music, for example, must take into account the milieu from which they spring. Such study, in fact, has already made useful contributions to the understanding of that milieu. But historians in the past have abandoned the study of society to sociologists, whose work at its best reveals a keen historical awareness but more often slights the dimension of time. The shelves have been loaded with studies of local communities, but there is nothing yet to compare with the historical studies of colonial New England community and family life nor with Stephan A. Thernstrom's study of Newburyport, Massachusetts, which explored the reality of the myth of upward mobility for that one community. We do not really know, for example, how many southerners found an avenue of upward mobility through the textile mill and how many never found the way up and out in later generations.

The family, Francis Butler Simkins once wrote, "was the core of Southern society; within its bounds everything worth while took place." Yet there is little historical literature on the family or such related topics as child-rearing practices and the sex roles of men and women. There have been good beginnings on the expanding public roles of middle-class women but little on the life and labor of the common sort beyond Julia Cherry Spruill's *Women's Life and Work in the Southern Colonies*. Indeed, ignorance abounds on the work habits of southerners. Whether the good old boy is really imbued with the work ethic or just bent on raising hell, or both, is hard to say. We know that blacks have always thought whites lazy, and vice versa, but we have little idea of the degree to which either may be right—or, what is more to the point, of the historical influences which have affected work habits. The study of diet, moreover, may offer useful clues to ethnic and regional boundaries. One sure test used to be the line beyond which one ordered grits for breakfast but instead got a greasy lump of cholesterol under the euphemism of hashed browns, but that atrocity, alas, is now commonly committed below the Potomac.

Most southern historians have taken some notice of

the church, but the history of religion has only begun to emerge from the stage of the medieval chronicle. Flannery O'Connor once wrote: "Whenever I'm asked why Southern writers particularly have a penchant for writing about freaks, I say it is because we are still able to recognize one. To be able to recognize a freak, you have to have some conception of the whole man, and in the South the general conception of man is still, in the main, theological. . . . I think it is safe to say that while the South is hardly Christ-centered, it is most certainly Christ-haunted. The Southerner, who isn't convinced of it, is very much afraid that he may have been formed in the image and likeness of God." The southern church, Samuel S. Hill, Jr., tells us, is something unique in all Christendom in its single-minded focus on salvation, its sense of assurance, and its rejection or simple unawareness of other versions of Christian experience. It serves as one of the chief instruments of ethnic solidarity; it has governed thought; and its biblical strains reverberate in the rhetoric of the region. In southern elections the "old Bible hand" always holds an advantage. If the church is in cultural captivity, which is a common belief, the question remains open whether it is the church or the culture which is in captivity.

Most of my comments so far apply equally to the white South and the black South, for the cultural affinities are great. The renewed interest in African culture and history may eventually trace more transatlantic legacies than we have suspected. One expression of that interest is the formation of a Southern Association of Africanists. One of its goals, we may hope, will be the exploration of cultural ties between Africa and the South. So far, however, little has been found to equal the visible African influences in Latin America and the West Indies or to equal the continuing identification with black Africa that has nourished the social myth of *négritude*. Whatever African traits endure, black Americans like other ethnic groups have an American experience and an American identity not shared by their cousins who were left behind. *Négritude* may evoke echoes of Africa, but "soul" evokes echoes of the South.

Ralph Ellison once wrote, moreover, that "southern whites cannot walk, talk, sing, conceive of laws or justice, think of sex, love, the family or freedom without responding to the presence of Negroes." Three and a half centuries of confrontation upon the southern soil have marked the culture of both black and white. The experience of each, while different, has touched the experience of the other. Like other aspects of ethnicity, this becomes most apparent when either group moves north and encounters the selfsame response that greeted earlier migrants from the Habsburg and Romanov empires. For both groups bring in their train that final indignity, that ultimate doom—the "southernization" of the North.

When black militants begin to put on dark glasses and menacing mannerisms, therefore, Glazer and Moynihan take notice that "the Southern style is now being brought into the North. . . . Violence is beginning to play a frightening role in politics. The demand for a rigid line between the races is now raised again, more strongly from the black side, this time." There had occurred a curious inversion, they said. The new practice of "mau-mauing the flak catchers" simply inverted an old southern habit of bulldozing the darkies. "The 'nigger' speech of the Georgia legislature became the 'honky' speech of the Harlem street corner, or the national television studio, complete with threats of violence."

To press the analogy further, the quest for "black power" might evoke memories of another quest for minority power: for local self-determination, for the concurrent majority, for constitutional guarantees—and the final desperate plunge into secession (the operative word now being separatism). The parallels, if not exact, are at least suggestive. "'Black pride,'" John Reed has suggested, "translates as the proposition that a man should be proud of what he is—which might appeal to a people as idiosyncratic, and proud of it, as white Southerners. 'Black power' can mean simply self-determination and freedom from outside meddling—another down home note. And the abandonment of nonviolence seems to mean that if someone is pushing you around, you hit him—the time-honored Southern white response, and one that may strain . . . empathic powers less than did saintly self-restraint."

It is scarcely a new finding that southerners white and black share the bonds of a common heritage, indeed a common tragedy, and often speak a common language, however seldom they may acknowledge it. But in this connection and countless others the idea of ethnicity affords historians a strategic vantage point from which to reassess the southern past. If we accept the ethnic analogy as a device serving to stimulate investigation and discovery, we can probably discount the danger that southern historians will be overwhelmed by the marvelous discovery that their field of study is nothing more or less than the formation of ethnic groups.

If we can remember that all humans are finite and different, but alike in having limitations, we can perhaps also discount the danger that the ethnic analogy will only reinforce old habits of seeking scapegoats and finding motes in the eyes of others. We cannot discount the possibility, however, that, like Frederick Jackson Turner writing about the frontier or Vann Woodward writing about Jim Crow, we have a heightened awareness of something that is passing away. Change is manifest and undeniable—certainly in Atlanta, the new Babylon on the Chattahoochee, the "city too busy to hate"—and our whole ethnic life may be flashing in front of our eyes just before we sink finally into the mainstream, never to rise again. Yet we learn time and again from the southern past and the history of others that to change is not necessarily to disappear. And we learn from modern psychology that to change is not necessarily to lose one's identity; to change, sometimes, is to find it.

2

Mythology: A New Frontier
in Southern History

THE IDEA OF THE SOUTH—OR MORE APPROPRIATELY, THE ideas of the South—belong in large part to the order of social myth. There are few areas of the modern world that have bred a regional mythology so potent, so profuse and diverse, even so paradoxical, as the American South. But the various mythical images of the South that have so significantly affected American history have yet to be subjected to the kind of broad and imaginative historical analysis that has been applied to the idea of the American West, particularly in Henry Nash Smith's *Virgin Land: The American West as Symbol and Myth*. The idea of the South has yet to be fully examined in the context of mythology, as essentially a problem of intellectual history.

To place the ideas of the South in the context of mythology, of course, is not necessarily to pass judgment upon them as illusions. The game of debunking myths, Harry Levin has warned us, starts "in the denunciation of myth as falsehood from the vantage-point of a rival myth." Mythology has other meanings, not all of them pejorative, and myths have a life of their own which to some degree renders irrelevant the question of their correlation to empirical fact. Setting aside for the moment the multiple connotations of the term, we may say that social myths in general, including those of the South, are simply mental pictures that portray the pattern of what a people think they are (or ought to be) or what somebody else thinks they are. They tend to develop abstract ideas in more or less concrete and dramatic terms. In the words of Henry Nash Smith, they fuse "concept and emotion into an image."

They may serve a variety of functions. "A myth," Mark Schorer has observed, "is a large, controlling image that gives philosophical meaning to the facts of ordinary life; that is, which has organizing value for experience." It may offer useful generalizations by which data may be tested. But being also "charged with values, aspirations, ideals and meanings," myths may become the ground for belief, for either loyalty and defense on the one hand or hostility and opposition on the other. In such circumstances a myth itself becomes one of the realities of history, significantly influencing the course of human action, for good or ill. There is, of course, always a danger of illusion, a danger that in ordering one's vision of reality, the myth may predetermine the categories of perception, rendering one blind to things that do not fit into the mental image.

Since the southern mind is reputed to be peculiarly resistant to pure abstraction and more receptive to the concrete and dramatic image, it may be unusually susceptible to mythology. Perhaps for the same reason our subject can best be approached through reference to the contrasting experiences of two southerners.

The first is the experience of a contemporary Louisiana writer, John T. Westbrook.

> During the thirties and early forties [Westbrook has written] when I was an English instructor at the University of Missouri, I was often mildly irritated by the average northerner's Jeeter-Lester-and-potlikker idea of the South. Even today the northern visitor inertia-headedly maintains his misconception: he hankers to see eroded hills and rednecks, scrub cotton and sharecropper shacks.
>
> It little profits me to drive him through Baton Rouge, show him the oil-ethyl-rubber-aluminum-chemical miles of industry along the Mississippi River, and say, "This . . . is the fastest-growing city of over 100,000 in America. We can amply substantiate our claim that we are atomic target number one, that in the next war the Russians will obliterate us first. . . ."
>
> Our northerner is suspicious of all this crass evidence presented to his senses. It bewilders and befuddles him. He is too deeply steeped in William Faulkner and Robert Penn Warren. The fumes of progress are in his nose and the bright steel of indusry towers before his eyes, but his heart is away in Yoknapatawpha County with razorback hogs and night riders. On this trip to the South he wants, above all else, to sniff the effluvium of backwoods-and-sand-hill subhumanity and to see at least one barn burn at midnight. So he looks at me with crafty misgiving, as if to say, "Well, you *do* drive a Cadillac, talk rather glibly about Kierkegaard and Sartre . . . but, after all, you *are* only fooling, aren't you? You do, don't you, sometimes, go out secretly by owl-light to drink swamp water and feed on sowbelly and collard greens?"

The other story is the experience of a southern historian, Frank L. Owsley, who traveled during World War I from Chicago via Cincinnati to Montgomery with a group of young ladies on the way to visit their menfolk at an army camp. He wrote later that, "despite every-thing which had ever been said to the contrary," the young ladies had a romantic conception of the "Sunny South" and looked forward to the journey with consid-erable excitement. "They expected to enter a pleasant land of white columned mansions, green pastures, ex-pansive cotton and tobacco fields where negroes sang spirituals all the day through." Except in the bluegrass basins of central Kentucky and Tennessee, what they actually found "were gutted hill-sides; scrub oak and pine; bramble and blackberry thickets, bottom lands once fertile now senile and exhausted, with spindling tobacco, corn, or cotton stalks ... unpainted houses which were hardly more than shacks or here and there the crumbling ruins of old mansions covered with briars, the homes of snakes and lizards." The disap-pointment of Dr. Owsley's ladies was, no doubt, even greater than that of Mr. Westbrook's friend in Baton Rouge.

There is a striking contrast between these two epi-sodes, both in the picture of southern reality and in the differing popular images that they present. The fact that they are four decades apart helps to account for the discrepancies, but what is not apparent at first is the common ancestry of the two images. They are not very distant cousins, collateral descendants from the standard image of the Old South, the plantation myth. The ver-sion of Owsley's lady friends is closer to the original primogenitor, which despite its advancing age and de-bility, still lives amid a flourishing progeny of legendary southern gentility. According to Francis Pendleton Gaines, author of *The Southern Plantation*, the pattern appeared full-blown at least as early as 1832 in John

Pendleton Kennedy's romance, *Swallow Barn*. It has had
a long career in story and novel and song, in the drama
and motion picture. The corrosions of age seem to have
ended its Hollywood career, although the old films still
turn up on the late late. It may still be found in the tour-
ist bait of shapely beauties in hoop skirts posed against
the backdrop of white columns at Natchez, Orton, or a
hundred other places.

These pictures are enough to trigger in the mind the
whole euphoric pattern of kindly old marster with his
mint julep; happy darkies singing in fields perpetually
white to the harvest or, as the case may be, sadly recall-
ing the long lost days of old; coquettish belles wooed by
slender gallants in gray underneath the moonlight and
magnolias. It is a pattern that yields all too easily to cari-
cature and ridicule, for in its more sophisticated versions the figure of the planter carries a heavy freight of
the aristocratic virtues: courtliness, grace, hospitality,
honor, *noblesse oblige*, as well as many no less charming
aristocratic vices: a lordly indifference to the balance
sheet, hot temper, profanity, overindulgence, a certain
stubborn obstinacy. The old-time Negro, when not a
figure of comedy, is the very embodiment of loyalty.
And the southern belle: "Beautiful, graceful, accomplished in social charm, bewitching in coquetry, yet
strangely steadfast in soul," Gaines has written, "she is
perhaps the most winsome figure in the whole field of
our fancy." "The plantation romance," Gaines says,
"remains our chief social idyl of the past; of an Arcadian
scheme of existence, less material, less hurried, less pro-
saically equalitarian, less futile, richer in picturesque-
ness, festivity, in realized pleasure that recked not of
hope or fear or unrejoicing labor."

But there is still more to the traditional pattern. Somewhere off in the piney woods and erosion-gutted clay hills, away from the white columns and gentility, there existed po' white trash: the crackers; hillbillies; sand-hillers; rag, tag, and bobtail; squatters; "po' buckra" to the Negroes; the Ransy Sniffle of A. B. Longstreet's *Georgia Scenes* and his literary descendants like Jeeter Lester and Ab Snopes, abandoned to poverty and degeneracy—the victims, it was later discovered, of hookworm, malaria, and pellagra. Somewhere in the pattern the respectable small farmer was lost from sight. He seemed to be neither romantic nor outrageous enough to fit in. His neglect provides the classic example in southern history of the blind spots engendered by the power of mythology. It was not until the 1930s that Frank L. Owsley and his students at Vanderbilt rediscovered the southern yeoman farmer as the characteristic, or at least the most numerous, antebellum white southerner. More about the yeoman presently; neglected in the plantation myth, he was in the foreground of another.

In contrast to the legitimate heirs of the plantation myth, the image of John T. Westbrook's Yankee visitor in Baton Rouge seems to be descended from what might be called the illegitimate line of the plantation myth, out of abolition. It is one of the ironies of our history that, as Gaines put it, the "two opposing sides of the fiercest controversy that ever shook national thought agreed concerning certain picturesque elements of plantation life and joined hands to set the conception unforgettably in public consciousness." The abolitionists found it difficult, or even undesirable, to escape the standard image. It was pretty fully developed even in

Uncle Tom's Cabin. Harriet Beecher Stowe made her villain a Yankee overseer, and has been accused by at least one latter-day abolitionist of implanting deeply in the American mind the stereotype of the faithful darkey. For others the plantation myth simply appeared in reverse, as a pattern of corrupt opulence resting upon human exploitation. Gentle old marster became the arrogant, haughty, imperious potentate, the very embodiment of sin, the central target of the antislavery attack. He maintained a seraglio in the slave quarters; he bred Negroes like cattle and sold them down the river to certain death in the sugar mills, separating families if that served his purpose, while southern women suffered in silence the guilty knowledge of their men's infidelity. The happy darkies in this picture became white men in black skins, an oppressed people longing for freedom, the victims of countless atrocities so ghastly as to be unbelievable except for undeniable evidence, forever seeking an opportunity to follow the North Star to freedom. The masses of the white folks were simply poor whites, relegated to ignorance and degeneracy by the slavocracy.

Both lines of the plantation myth have been remarkably prolific, but the more adaptable one has been that of the abolitionists. It has repeatedly readjusted to new conditions while the more legitimate line has courted extinction, running out finally into the decadence perpetrated by Tennessee Williams. Meanwhile, the abolitionist image of brutality persisted through and beyond Reconstruction in the Republican outrage mills and bloody shirt political campaigns. For several decades it was more than overbalanced by the southern image of

Reconstruction horrors, disarmed by prophets of a New South created in the image of the North, and almost completely submerged under the popularity of plantation romances in the generation before Owsley's trainload of ladies ventured into their "Sunny South" of the teens. At about that time, however, the undercurrents began to emerge once again into the mainstream of American thought. In the clever decade of the twenties a kind of neo-abolitionist myth of the Savage South was compounded. It seemed that the benighted South, after a period of relative neglect, suddenly became an object of concern to every publicist in the country. One southern abomination after another was ground through their mills: child labor, peonage, lynching, hookworm, pellagra, the Scopes trial, the fundamentalist crusade against Al Smith. The guiding genius was H. L. Mencken, the hatchet man from Baltimore who developed the game of South baiting into a national pastime, a fine art at which he had no peer. In 1917, when he started constructing his image of "Baptist and Methodist barbarism" below the Potomac, he began with the sterility of southern literature and went on from there. With characteristic glee he anointed one J. Gordon Coogler of South Carolina "the last bard of Dixie" and quoted his immortal couplet:

> Alas, for the South! Her books have grown fewer—
> She never was much given to literature.

"Down there," Mencken wrote, "a poet is now almost as rare as an oboe-player, a dry-point etcher or metaphysician." As for "critics, musical composers, painters, sculptors, architects . . . there is not even a bad one between the Potomac mud-flats and the Gulf. Nor an historian. Nor a sociologist. Nor a philosopher. Nor a theologian. Nor a scientist. In all these fields the south is an awe-inspiring blank." It was as complete a vacuity as the interstellar spaces, this "Sahara of the Bozart," the "Bible Belt." The South, in short, had fallen prey to its poor whites, who would soon achieve apotheosis in the Snopes family.

It did not end with the twenties. The image was reinforced by a variety of episodes: the Scottsboro trials, chain gang exposés, Bilbo and Rankin, Senate filibusters, labor wars; much later by Central High and Orval Faubus, Emmett Till and Autherine Lucy and James Meredith, bus boycotts and freedom riders; and not least of all by the lush growth of literature that covered Mencken's Sahara, with Erskine Caldwell's *Tobacco Road* and Faulkner's *Sanctuary* and various other products of what Ellen Glasgow labeled the southern gothic and a less elegant Mississippi editor called the "privy school" of literature. In the words of Faulkner's character, Gavin Stevens, the North suffered from a curious "gullibility: a volitionless, almost helpless capacity and eagerness to believe anything about the South not even provided it be derogatory but merely bizarre enough and strange enough." And Faulkner, to be sure, did not altogether neglect that market. Not surprisingly, he was taken in some quarters for a realist, and the image of southern savagery long obscured the critics' recognition of his manifold merits.

The family line of the plantation myth can be traced only so far in the legendary gentility and savagery of

the South. Other family lines seem to be entirely independent—if sometimes on friendly terms. In *The New
South Creed*, Paul M. Gaston has traced the evolution
of the creed into a genuine myth. In the aftermath of
the Civil War, apostles of a "New South," led by Henry
W. Grady, preached with almost evangelical fervor the
gospel of industry. Their dream, Gaston writes, "was
essentially a promise of American life for the South. It
proffered all the glitter and glory and freedom from
guilt that inhered in the American ideal." From advocacy, from this vision of the future, the prophets soon
advanced to the belief that "their promised land [was]
at hand, no longer merely a gleaming goal." "By the
twentieth century . . . there was established for many in
the South a pattern of belief within which they could
see themselves and their section as rich, success-
oriented, and just . . . opulence and power were at hand
. . . the Negro lived in the best of all possible worlds."

As the twentieth century advanced, and wealth did in
fact increase, the creed of the New South took on an
additional burden of crusades for good roads and education, blending them into what Francis B. Simkins has
called the "trinity of Southern progress": industrial
growth, good roads, and schools. When the American
Historical Association went to Durham in 1929 for its
annual meeting, Robert D. W. Connor of the University
of North Carolina presented the picture of a rehabili-
tated South that had "shaken itself free from its heritage
of war and Reconstruction. Its self-confidence restored,
its political stability assured, its prosperity regained,
its social problems on the way to solution. . . ." Two

months before Connor spoke, the New York Stock Exchange had broken badly, and in the aftermath the image he described was seriously blurred, but before the end of the thirties it was being brought back into focus by renewed industrial expansion that received increased momentum from World War II and postwar prosperity.

Two new and disparate images emerged in the depression years, both with the novel feature of academic trappings and affiliations. One was the burgeoning school of sociological regionalism led by Howard W. Odum and Rupert B. Vance at the University of North Carolina. It was neither altogether the image of the Savage South nor that of industrial progress, although both entered into the compound. It was rather a concept of the "Problem South," which Franklin D. Roosevelt labeled "the Nation's Economic Problem No. 1," a region with indisputable shortcomings but with potentialities that needed constructive attention and the application of rational social planning. Through the disciples of Odum as well as the agencies of the New Deal, the vision issued in a flood of social science monographs and programs for reform and development. To one Chapel Hill undergraduate at the time, it seemed in retrospect that "we had more of an attitude of service to the South as the South than was true later."

The regionalists were challenged by the Vanderbilt Agrarians, who developed a myth of the traditional South. Their manifesto, *I'll Take My Stand*, by Twelve Southerners, appeared by fortuitous circumstance in 1930 when industrial capitalism seemed on the verge of collapse. In reaction against both the progressive New South and Mencken's image of savagery they champi-

oned, in Donald Davidson's words, a "traditional society
. . . that is stable, religious, more rural than urban, and
politically conservative," in which human needs were
supplied by "family, bloodkinship, clanship, folkways,
custom, community." The ideal of the traditional virtues
took on the texture of myth in their image of the agrarian South. Of course, in the end, their agrarianism
proved less important as a social-economic force than as
a context for creative literature. The central figures in
the movement were the Fugitive poets John Crowe Ran-
som, Donald Davidson, Allen Tate, and Robert Penn
Warren. But, as Louis Rubin has emphasized, "Through
their vision of an agrarian community, the authors of
I'll Take My Stand presented a critique of the modern
world. In contrast to the hurried, nervous life of cities,
the image of the agrarian South was of a life in which
human beings existed serenely and harmoniously."
Their critique of the modern frenzy "has since been
echoed by commentator after commentator."

While it never became altogether clear whether the
Agrarians were celebrating the aristocratic graces or following the old Jeffersonian dictum that "Those who
labor in the earth are the chosen people of God," most
of them seemed to come down eventually on the side of
the farmer rather than the planter. Frank L. Owsley,
who rediscovered the antebellum yeoman farmer, was
one of them. Insofar as they extolled the yeoman farmer, the Agrarians laid hold upon an image older than
any of the others—the Jeffersonian South. David M.
Potter, a southerner then in exile at Stanford University, remarked in 1961 how difficult it was for many people to realize that the benighted South "was, until recently, regarded by many liberals as the birthplace and

the natural bulwark of the Jeffersonian ideal." The theme has long had an appeal for historians as well as others. Frederick Jackson Turner developed it for the West and William E. Dodd for the South. According to Dodd the democratic, equalitarian South of the Jeffersonian image was the norm; the plantation slavocracy was the great aberration. Dodd's theme has been reflected in the writing of other historians, largely in terms of a region subjected to economic colonialism by an imperial Northeast: Charles A. Beard, for example, who saw the sectional conflict as a struggle between agrarianism and industrialism; Howard K. Beale, who interpreted Reconstruction in similar terms; C. Vann Woodward, defender of populism; Arthur S. Link, who first rediscovered the southern progressives; and Walter Prescott Webb, who found the nation divided between an exploited South and West on the one hand, and a predatory Northeast on the other. Jefferson, like the South, it sometimes seems, can mean all things to all men, and the Jefferson image of agrarian democracy has been a favorite recourse of southern liberals, just as his states' rights doctrines have nourished conservatism.

In stark contrast to radical agrarianism there stands the concept of monolithic conservatism in southern politics. It seems to be a proposition generally taken for granted now that the South is, by definition, conservative—and always has been. Yet the South in the late nineteenth century produced some of the most radical Populists and in the twentieth was a bulwark of Wilsonian progressivism and Roosevelt's New Deal, at least up to a point. A good case has been made by Arthur S. Link that southern agrarian radicals pushed Wilson further into progressivism than he intended to go. During the twenties southern minority leadership in Congress kept up such a running battle against the conservative tax policies of Andrew Mellon that, believe it or not, there was real fear among some northern businessmen during the 1932 campaign that Franklin D. Roosevelt might be succeeded by that radical southern income-taxer, John Nance Garner! The conservative image of course has considerable validity, but it obscures understanding of such phenomena as Albert Gore, Russell Long, Lister Hill, John Sparkman, Olin D. Johnston, William Fulbright, the Yarboroughs of Texas, or the late Estes Kefauver. In the 1960 campaign the conservative image seriously victimized Lyndon B. Johnson, who started in politics as a vigorous New Dealer and later maneuvered through the Senate the first civil rights legislation since Reconstruction.

The infinite variety of southern mythology could be cataloged and analyzed endlessly. A suggestive list would include the proslavery South; the Confederate South; the demagogic South; the states' rights South; the fighting South; the lazy South; the folklore South; the South of jazz and the blues; the booster South; the rapacious South running away with northern industries; the liberal South of the interracial movement; the white supremacy South of racial segregation, which seems to be for some the all-encompassing "southern way of life"; the Anglo-Saxon (or was it the Scotch-Irish?) South, the most American of all regions because of its native population; or the internationalist South, a mainstay of the Wilson, Roosevelt, and Truman foreign policies.

The South, then, has been the seedbed for a proliferation of paradoxical myths, all of which have some basis in empirical fact and all of which doubtlessly have, or have had, their true believers. The result has been, in David Potter's words, that the South has become an enigma, "a kind of Sphinx on the American land." What is really the answer to the riddle, what is at bottom the foundation of southern distinctiveness has never been established with finality, but the quest for a central theme of southern history has repeatedly engaged the region's historians. Like Frederick Jackson Turner, who extracted the essential West in his frontier thesis, southern historians have sought to distill the quintessence of the South into some kind of central theme.

In a 1962 survey of these efforts David L. Smiley of Wake Forest College has concluded that they turn upon two basic lines of thought: "the causal effects of environment, and the development of certain acquired characteristics of the people called Southern." The distinctive climate and weather of the South, it has been argued, slowed the pace of life, tempered the speech of the South, dictated the system of staple crops and Negro slavery—in short, predetermined the plantation economy. The more persuasive suggestions have resulted from concentration upon human factors and causation. The best known is that set forth by Ulrich B. Phillips. The quintessence of southernism, he wrote in 1928, was "a common resolve indomitably maintained" that the South "shall be and remain a white man's country." Whether "expressed with the frenzy of a demagogue or maintained with a patrician's quietude," this was "the cardinal test of a Southerner and the central theme of Southern history." Other historians have pointed to the rural nature of southern society as the basic conditioning factor, to the prevalence of the country gentleman ideal imported from England, to the experience of the

South as a conscious minority unified by criticism and attack from outside, to the fundamental piety of the Bible Belt, and to various other factors. It has even been suggested by one writer that a chart of the mule population would determine the boundaries of the South.

More recently, two historians have attempted new explanations. In his search for a southern identity, C. Vann Woodward advances several crucial factors: the experience of poverty in a land of plenty; failure and defeat in a land that glorifies success; sin and guilt amid the legend of American innocence; and a sense of place and belonging among a people given to abstraction. David M. Potter, probing the enigma of the South, has found the key to the riddle in the prevalence of a folk society. "This folk culture, we know, was far from being ideal or utopian," he writes, "and was in fact full of inequality and wrong, but if the nostalgia persists was it because even the inequality and wrong were parts of a life that still had a relatedness and meaning which our more bountiful life in the mass culture seems to lack?"

It is significant that both explanations are expressed largely in the past tense, Potter's explicitly in terms of nostalgia. They recognize, by implication at least, still another image—that of the dynamic, or changing, South. The image may be rather nebulous and the ultimate ends unclear, but the fact of change is written inescapably across the southern scene. The consciousness of change has been present so long as to become in itself one of the abiding facts of southern life. As far back as the twenties it was the consciousness of change that quickened the imaginations of a cultivated and sensitive minority, giving us the Southern Renaissance in literature. The peculiar historical consciousness of the southern writer, Allen Tate suggested, "made possible the curious burst of intelligence that we get at a crossing of the ways, not unlike, on an infinitesimal scale, the outburst of poetic genius at the end of the sixteenth century when commercial England had already begun to crush feudal England." Trace it through modern southern writing, and at the center—in Ellen Glasgow, in Faulkner, Wolfe, Caldwell, the Fugitive-Agrarian poets, and all the others—there is the consciousness of change, of suspension between two worlds, a double focus looking both backward and forward.

The southerner of the present generation has seen the old landmarks crumble with great rapidity: the one-crop agriculture and the very predominance of agriculture itself, the one-party system, the white primary, the poll tax, racial segregation, the poor white (at least in his classic connotations), the provincial isolation—virtually all the foundations of the established order. Yet, sometimes, the old traditions endure in surprising new forms. Southern folkways have been carried even into the factory, and the Bible Belt has revealed resources undreamed of in Mencken's philosophy—but who, in the twenties, could have anticipated Martin Luther King?

One wonders what new images, what new myths, might be nurtured by the emerging South. Some, like Harry Ashmore, have merely written *An Epitaph for Dixie*. It is the conclusion of two southern sociologists, John M. Maclachlan and Joe S. Floyd, Jr., that present trends "might well hasten the day when the South, once perhaps the most distinctively 'different' American region, will have become . . . virtually indistinguishable from the other urban-industrial areas of the nation." Phillips long ago suggested that the disappearance of race as a major issue would end southern distinctiveness. One may wonder if southern distinctiveness might even be preserved in new conditions entirely antithetic to his image. Charles L. Black, Jr., another *émigré* southerner (at Yale Law School) has confessed to a fantastic dream that southern whites and Negroes, bound in a special bond of common tragedy, may come to recognize their kinship. There is not the slightest warrant for it, he admits, in history, sociology, or common sense. But if it should come to pass, he suggests, "The South, which has always felt itself reserved for a high destiny, would have found it, and would have come to flower at last. And the fragrance of it would spread, beyond calculation, over the world."

Despite the consciousness of change, perhaps even more because of it, southerners still feel a persistent pull toward identification with their native region as a ground for belief and loyalty. Is there not yet something more than nostalgia to the idea of the South? Is there not some living heritage with which the modern southerner can identify? Is there not, in short, a viable myth of the South? The quest for myth has been a powerful factor in recent southern literature, and the suspicion is strong that it will irresistibly affect any historian's quest for the central theme of southern history. It has all too clearly happened before—in the climatic theory, for example, which operated through its geographical determinism to justify the social order of the plantation, or the Phillips thesis of white supremacy, which has become almost a touchstone of the historian's attitude toward the whole contemporary issue of race. "To elaborate a central theme," David L. Smiley has asserted, is "but to reduce a multi-faceted story to a single aspect, and its result . . . but to find new footnotes to confirm revealed truths and prescribed views." The trouble is that the quest for the central theme, like Turner's frontier thesis, becomes absorbed willy-nilly into the process of myth making.

To pursue the Turner analogy a little further, the conviction grows that the frontier thesis, with all its elaborations and critiques, has been exhausted (and in part exploded) as a source of new historical insight. It is no derogation of insights already gained to suggest that the same thing has happened to the quest for the central theme, and that the historian, *as historian*, may be better able to illuminate our understanding of the South now by turning to a new focus upon the regional mythology.

Undertaking the analysis of mythology will no longer require him to venture into uncharted wilderness. A substantial conceptual framework of mythology has already been developed by anthropologists, philosophers, psychologists, theologians, and literary critics. The historian, while his field has always been closely related to mythology, has come only lately to the critique of it. But there now exists a considerable body of historical literature on the American national mythology and the related subject of the national character, and Smith's stimulating *Virgin Land* suggests the trails that may be followed into the idea of the South.

Several trails, in fact, have already been blazed. In 1925 Francis Pendleton Gaines successfully traced the rise and progress of the plantation myth, and two more-recent authors belatedly took to the same trail. Howard

R. Floan considerably increased our knowledge of the abolitionist version in his study of northern writers, *The South in Northern Eyes*, while William R. Taylor approached the subject from an entirely new perspective in his *Cavalier and Yankee*. Shields McIlwaine has traced the literary image of the poor white, while Stanley Elkins' *Slavery* has broken sharply from established concepts on both sides of that controversial question. One foray into the New South has been made in Paul Gaston's *The New South Creed*. Yet many important areas— the Confederate and Reconstruction myths, for example—still remain almost untouched.

Some of the basic questions that need to be answered have been attacked in these studies; some have not. It is significant that students of literature have led the way and have pointed up the value of even third-rate creative literature in the critique of myth. The historian, however, should be able to contribute other perspectives. With his peculiar time perspective he can seek to unravel the tangled genealogy of myth that runs back from the modern changing South to Jefferson's yeoman and Kennedy's plantation. Along the way he should investigate the possibility that some obscure dialectic may be at work in the pairing of obverse images: the two versions of the plantation, New South and Old, Cavalier and Yankee, genteel and savage, regionalist and agrarian, nativist and internationalist.

What, the historian may ask, have been the historical origins and functions of the myths? The plantation myth, according to Gaines and Floan, was born in the controversy and emotion of the struggle over slavery. It had polemical uses for both sides. Taylor, on the other hand, finds its origin in the psychological need, both

North and South, to find a corrective for the grasping, materialistic, rootless society symbolized by the image of the Yankee. Vann Woodward and Gaston have noted its later psychological uses in bolstering the morale of the New South. The image of the Savage South has obvious polemical uses, but has it not others? Has it not served the function of national catharsis? Has it not created for many Americans a convenient scapegoat upon which the sins of all may be symbolically laid and thereby expiated—a most convenient escape from problem solving? To what extent, indeed, has the mythology of the South in general welled up from the subconscious depths? Taylor, especially, has emphasized this question, but the skeptical historian will also be concerned with the degree to which it has been the product or the device of deliberate manipulation by propagandists and vested interests seeking identification with the "real" South.

Certainly any effort to delineate the unique character of a people must take into account its mythology. "Poets," James G. Randall suggested, "have done better in expressing this oneness of the South than historians in explaining it." Can it be that the historians have been looking in the wrong places, that they have failed to seek the key to the enigma where the poets have so readily found it—in the mythology that has had so much to do with shaping character, unifying society, developing a sense of community, of common ideals and shared goals, making the region conscious of its distinctiveness? Perhaps by turning to different and untrodden paths we shall encounter the central theme of southern history at last on the new frontier of mythology.

3

The Benighted South: Origins of a Modern Image

WE SOUTHERNERS, JONATHAN DANIELS ONCE SAID, ARE "A mythological people, created half out of dream and half out of slander, who live in a still legendary land." Most Americans, including southerners, carry about with them an assorted mental baggage of southern mythology in which a variety of elements have been assembled: the Jeffersonian image of agrarian democracy, the progressive creed of the New South, the Vanderbilt Agrarian myth of the traditional South, the problem South of the regional sociologists, to mention a few. But the main burden of southern mythology is still carried in those unavoidable categories set by the nineteenth-century sectional conflict: the romantic plantation myth of gentility on the one hand and the obverse, if in many respects similar, abolitionist plantation myth of barbarity on the other.

Both versions have had a remarkable longevity; both may yet be encountered in literature and popular thought; both have been adaptable to new conditions;

but somewhere along the road to reunion the abolitionist version was outpaced by the myth of the New
South and the popularity of plantation romances. It was
not until the 1920s that a kind of neo-abolitionist image
of the benighted South was compounded out of elements both old and new into a mind-set that has influenced strongly the outlook of the twentieth century.

The background for the newer and more complex
image was what Hamlin Garland called after a southern
visit in 1919 "an unlovely time of sorry transition." As
the postwar South of the 1920s surged into a strange
new world of urban booms and farm distress, it found
itself on a strange and unfamiliar terrain of diversity
and change in which there lurked a thousand hazards
to the older orthodoxies. Reaction to the new circumstances made it a time when, in Howard Odum's words,
the South was swept into a "state of mind similar to that
commonly manifest in war times. . . . During the Ku
Klux era one was advised that it was better to keep one's
mouth shut on all debatable issues because one never
knew who was around."

The defensive temper of the 1920s, to be sure, was
not altogether a southern phenomenon. Over the first
two decades of the century there had been an increasing
tendency to associate American nationalism with nativism, Anglo-Saxon racism, and militant Protestantism.
The South was in the vanguard of the new development, with all the enthusiasm of a recent convert. By the
1920s nativism in the South had become a peculiar expression of sectionalism in terms of American nationalism. If the test of Americanism was native birth of
Anglo-Saxon ancestry, it followed that the South was the
"most American" of all regions. "One of the glories of

the South," the *Manufacturers Record* boasted, "is that its foreign stock is so limited as compared with that of other sections." But if in adopting Anglo-Saxon nativism the white South was largely importing a creed that fulfilled ancient urges, it was soon developing to a new intensity the anti-Catholic and anti-Semitic corollaries and reexporting nativism with the addition of certain historic southern trappings in the new Ku Klux Klan.

Fundamentalism, the other great defensive movement of the day, had obvious similarities to the Klan. While there were no organic links between the two, more than one klansman found his Anglo-Saxon nativism and his fear of the Roman menace reinforced from the Protestant pulpit. One of the classic tributes to the newest chosen race had been penned by Methodist Bishop Warren A. Candler of Georgia in his *Great Revivals and the Great Republic*, which revealed the Anglo-Saxons to be divinely appointed for the advancement of evangelical religion in the world, a theme reechoed time and again by preachers and revivalists. From there it was not far to sectionalism. Other regions, a Baptist divine noted, had lost "whatever there is of advantage in this unmixed Anglo-Saxon blood." Romanism had flooded their cities and had "invaded and despoiled the old patriotism and the old culture and political ideals." The logic was inescapable. "The hope of the world is America, the hope of America is evangelical religion of the most orthodox type, the hope of the American church is the Southern Evangelical churches."

Unfortunately, however, the serpent of rationalism had already entered the southern Eden. The new temptations of evolution and the higher criticism had crept into the state universities, and Baptist leader Victor I.

Masters complained that not even the Christian schools
"have had altogether an easy time in safeguarding the
class rooms from the miasmatic utterances of teachers
who have been contaminated by the rationalistic and
evolutionary imaginings of the New Religion."

With the dawning recognition that new theories were
influencing the colleges and schools, even the pulpit,
orthodoxy emerged into a new militancy with the fundamentalist movement, and by that mysterious process
through which complex problems become simplified
into symbolic issues, the defense of the fundamentalist
faith came somehow to rest upon opposition to Darwinism. The movement found its peerless leader in William
Jennings Bryan, who in his lectures against Darwinism
was already by 1920 on the high road to his great pyr-
rhic victory at Dayton, Tennessee.

It was probably the Scopes trial of 1925 more than
any other single event that bore in upon the masses of
southerners the existence of a growing image of the
benighted South that contrasted so starkly with the special images they had of themselves as democratic agrarians, as progressive builders and developers, as "the
most American" of all Americans, as the defenders of
the faith. By contrast they read or heard accounts of
journalists attracted to the circus in Dayton that ranged
from disappointment to ridicule, from the judgment by
Joseph Wood Krutch that his native Tennessee was
victimized chiefly by the timidity of its intellectuals and
legislators to H. L. Mencken's columns cataloging "mo-
rons," "hill-billies," "peasants," and the "degraded non-
sense which country preachers are ramming and ham-
mering into yokel skulls."

The image by then was already virtually complete, and it had been rapidly compounded out of multiple elements within less than a decade. After some years of relative neglect, the South had suddenly become an object of concern to every publicist in the country. "It is difficult now," Gerald W. Johnson wrote in 1924, "to find on the news stands a serious magazine without an article on some phase of life below the Potomac, or a discussion of one idea or another that has come out of the South." After the dissolution of the Wilsonian synthesis in 1920 it seemed that great torrents of abuse and criticism were suddenly released upon the region. In fact, the infidels had crossed the Mason-Dixon line to establish their headquarters in Baltimore, whence H. L. Mencken directed a great campaign of South-baiting. The sage of Baltimore, of course, was a man of catholic taste in his choice of targets. From the aristocratic heights of the *Smart Set*, the *American Mercury*, and the *Sunpapers*, he chronicled the doings of *Homo Boobiens* everywhere, but with a special solicitude for the southern breed. Nearly all the major elements of his more fully developed image of the South were present in his first essay on the theme, "The Sahara of the Bozart," published in the New York *Evening Mail* in 1917 and later revised for *Smart Set* and *Prejudices*—but the emphasis at first was on the sterility of southern culture. It was "amazing to contemplate so vast a vacuity," he wrote. "One thinks of the interstellar spaces, of the colossal reaches of the now mythical ether. . . . It would be impossible in all history to match so complete a drying-up of civilization."

His genetic explanation of the southern plight owed

an interesting debt to the original plantation myth, and anticipated William Faulkner's saga of the Snopes family. Once there had been an aristocratic culture of the finest sort, his history went, but it had been left bleeding and helpless by the Civil War, which opened the way to the "lower orders" who had no more comprehension of the ancient faith "than any other like group of former plumbers, corner grocers, and crossroads lawyers." They were "eighth-rate men wearing the stolen coats of dead first-rate men." Their taste was "only a compound of elemental fears and appetites— chiefly the fear of ideas, and the appetite for security."

But the fundamental root of evil, and the most consistent target of Mencken's vilification, as time went by, was the peculiar clerical tyranny of "Baptist and Methodist barbarism" below the Potomac. "No bolder attempt to set up a theocracy was ever made in the world," he announced with typical hyperbole, "and none ever had behind it a more implacable fanaticism." The clerical will to power, culminating in the fundamentalist excesses of the 1920s, was also given a peculiarly Menckenesque history stemming from the Civil War. Numerous among the slackers and cowards, the preachers found themselves after the war the only survivors with any pretense of training. With little competition from the cultivated remnants of the Confederacy, they soon established a religious, cultural, and political hegemony. Ignorant even in their superiority to the "yowling yokels" over whom they held sway, they spread abroad their own obsessive fear of intelligence, the inquiring mind, or individual freedom. The climax came with prohibition, over which they gloated "in their remote

Methodist Tabernacles as they gloat over a hanging."
Intoxicated by that success, the Baptist and Methodist
shamans of the Bible Belt proceeded next "to put down
learning by the law." Professional defenders of the
South, their antennae delicately tuned to sectional
defamation, served with their responses only to publi-
cize their tormentor and add to his bumptious gaiety.
When Mencken wrote that he knew of New Yorkers
who had been in Cochin China, Kafiristan, Paraguay,
Somaliland, and even West Virginia, "but not one who
has ever penetrated the miasmatic jungles of Arkansas,"
a former governor retorted with an unconsciously ludicrous letter offering statistics on agricultural production
and a "two volume deluxe illustrated set of 'The Folklore of Arkansas'" as evidence of the state's cultural
achievements. Mencken merrily gathered and published
some of the prize castigations. "By cutting through six
inches of fat and drilling through four inches of bone,"
Fred Sullens raged in the Jackson *Daily News*, "one
might possibly find Mencken's brain cavity—but he
would not find any grey matter there." "This modern
Attila!" Clio Harper cried in the *Arkansas Writer*. "This
brachycephalous Caliban! The Black Knight of Slander!
An intellectual Houyhnhnm!" All of which only inspired
Mencken to further heights of calumny against the
South, the "bunghole of the United States, a cesspool
of Baptists, a miasma of Methodism, snake-charmers,
phoney real-estate operators, and syphilitic evangelists."

If Mencken was the guiding genius in creating the
new image of the benighted South, he was by no means
its only architect. While Mencken ran amok in Baltimore, other men of differing temperaments contributed

their own special perspectives. Two books significant in the developing pattern were published in 1924. William Henry Skaggs, a young progressive mayor of Talladega in the 1880s, a leading Alabama Populist in the 1890s, and subsequently a professional lecturer based in New York, set forth in *The Southern Oligarchy* what he called in his subtitle, *An Appeal in Behalf of the Silent Masses of Our Country Against the Despotic Rule of the Few*. In tones of righteous indignation, more redolent of abolition than of Mencken, and in lengthy catalogs of southern deficiencies like the later fashion of regional sociologists, Skaggs handed down one of the most thoroughgoing indictments of the region ever published, detailing at length political corruption, landlordism, illiteracy, peonage, lynch law, partisan and racial proscription, and a hundred other delinquencies. He "brought to his work wide reading, a formidable array of statistics and praiseworthy industry," one reviewer thought. "If he could have presented his material temperately he might have written a great and much needed book." As it was, the book poured vitriol so "liberally upon . . . the Southern princes, potentates and powers" that its impact was dissipated.

In contrast to Skaggs, Frank Tannenbaum, a young professor at Columbia University, brought together in his *Darker Phases of the South* a slender collection of essays that constituted one of the most perceptive social critiques of the times, more balanced and charitable in approach than Skaggs's book, but all the more damaging for its restraint. In successive chapters he considered the Ku Klux Klan, mill villages, prisons, tenancy, and the race question. The social setting for the development of the Klan he described as one of "historical ante-

cedents, passions, prejudices, hates, loves, ennui, the
need for constructing a defense mechanism against
one's own sins, the attempt to preserve as static what is
becoming dynamic, the craving for dramatization and
excitement in the face of a dull and monotonous existence." Boasting of its racial purity, the South had segregated and buried its Anglo-Saxons in the mill villages.
The history of southern prisons was one long story of
brutality, neglect, and indifference. The rural South
was afflicted with "a white plague—cotton," the source
of poverty, much of the race problem, soil exhaustion,
laziness, peonage, ignorance, and a dozen other shortcomings.

The grave social issues that troubled Skaggs and
Tannenbaum became perennial topics for publicists
and social scientists during the decade. For nearly a
month in 1921, for example, the New York *World* ran
a comprehensive exposé of the Ku Klux Klan, inadvertently contributing to its growth by the publicity. Although the Klan had become national in scope, its
southern origins gave it an important role in the pattern
of the benighted South. The cotton mills from the beginning of the century had been through a cycle of criticism that firmly established the stereotype of the mill
president as a greedy feudal baron. A second stage of
attack in the 1920s, of which Tannenbaum's book is one
example, dwelt upon the theme of the mill village and
corporate control that threatened to develop a socially
isolated and hereditary helot class. Though not unlike
earlier mill villages in Old and New England, the southern mill village, one writer says, took "its place in the
eyes of the Nation as one in a long procession of peculiar
characteristics of the South, along with slavery and cot-

ton, sharecropping and low incomes, race problems and demagogic Democracy."

The eternal race question had not yet been brought into the central focus of the image, but insofar as it appeared, it was in the most barbaric aspects. In the climate of a national consensus on white supremacy, the race issue of the 1920s was not an issue of segregation; it was an issue of lynching and peonage. In 1919 the National Association for the Advancement of Colored People (NAACP) sponsored a national conference on lynching that launched a drive for a federal antilynching bill and a publicity campaign, paralleled by efforts of the Commission on Interracial Cooperation, that lasted through a decade. In 1921 there came the first in a series of revolting disclosures of peonage and penal brutality, chiefly involving Negroes, when one John Williams on a farm near Covington, Georgia, murdered eleven Negroes in a vain effort to destroy the evidence that he was holding them in peonage. The episode of the "murder farm" was followed through the decade by other revelations of brutality toward prisoners, both in convict-lease camps and in state and county prisons.

In the South itself a fifth column of native Menckens and Tannenbaums contributed their own bit to the growing attack. Gerald W. Johnson of the Greensboro *Daily News* wielded perhaps the most trenchant style of the native critics both before and after he ascended unto the right hand of Mencken himself on the Baltimore *Sun*. "Too much has been said of the South's need for 'sympathetic criticism,'" Johnson complained. It needed no sympathy for bigotry, intolerance, superstition, and prejudice, but "criticism that is ruthless toward those things—bitter towards them, furiously against them—

and sympathetic only with its idealism, with its loyalty, with its courage and its inflexible determination." But he found grounds for hope. The Ku Klux Klan had served the useful purpose "of rousing the intelligence of the South to a realization of the thralldom under which it has lain."

Indeed, the incubator of the 1920s produced a sizable number of southern journalists who found an almost ridiculously simple formula for fame. Attack on the grotesqueries of the benighted South became for that decade a high road to the Pulitzer Prize. Three awards went for attacks on the Klan: in 1923 to the Memphis *Commercial Appeal* under C. P. J. Mooney; in 1926 to the Columbus *Enquirer-Sun* under Julian and Julia Collier Harris; and in 1928 to Grover C. Hall of the Montgomery *Advertiser*. Editorial prizes went in 1925 to Robert Lathan for an editorial in the Charleston *News and Courier* on the decline of southern statesmanship and in 1929 to Louis I. Jaffe of the Norfolk *Virginian-Pilot* for an editorial campaign against lynching. And these were only the most celebrated among the vigorous journalists who had shaken off the inclination "to accept traditional romanticism as established fact."

Well before the end of the 1920s, then, most of the factors in the new image of the benighted South had fallen into place, and its influence ran deep. A philosopher and critic, Eliseo Vivas, who had a later change of heart, wrote of what at the time he took the South to be: "It was the Bible belt, the land of the Klu [sic] Klux Klan, and I knew, knew with the confidence of a good 'liberal,' that nothing but fundamentalism and intolerance could come out of the South. No one around me would have thought it possible to challenge this proposition. It was part of a system of *idées reçues* that constituted the then reigning orthodoxy of my group." Donald Davidson wrote in the 1930s:

> The legend of the barbarism of the South . . . and of the vulgarity and dullness of the Middle West, for a good many years has governed the approach of the metropolitan East to the phenomena of life in the so-called hinterland. . . . The South—so the tale runs—is a region full of little else but lynchings, shootings, chain-gangs, poor whites, Ku Kluxers, hookworm, pellagra, and a few decayed patricians whose chief intent is to deprive the uncontaminated, spiritual-singing Negro of his life and liberty. But what is more shocking, it is inhabited by believers in God, who pass anti-evolution laws; and more shocking still, it is in thought and deed studiously backward and anti-progressive. . . . Over such pictures the East stormed, or shed crocodile tears, in the clever nineteen-twenties.

Davidson's summary was almost definitively complete. About the only things omitted were the tyrannies of prohibition and the mill village.

Identifying the causes and consequences of this phenomenon presents an intricate puzzle for the historian, one that challenges his resources of analysis and objectivity. The historical context in which it developed offers one fundamental explanation. A southern society that had remained comparatively static since Reconstruction suddenly felt itself caught up after World War I by the forces of change. The consciousness of change, the fears and defensiveness it aroused, gave increased power to what Wilbur J. Cash called the "savage ideal" of intolerance and repression, heightening both its aggressiveness and visibility. But such times of transition are inevitably times of conflict. For better or for worse, the genie of modernism was out of the bottle, and the very ferocity of Ku Kluxry and fundamentalism was the ferocity of those who were fighting another lost cause.

As the growing band of critics and social scientists began turning over the rocks in the sunny South, bringing its social ills out into the glare of daylight, the reform urge contributed significantly, if sometimes inadvertently, to the image of the benighted South. Even Mencken, who would have sunk into a purple dudgeon at the suggestion that he was associated with uplift, cannot wholly escape the charge. He was continually trying to nurture the critics and rebels of the New South.

Not least of all among the contemporary factors was the irreverent levity of the jazz age, finding its most bizarre expression in Mencken, an attitude of metropolitan sophistication that took jocular delight in baiting the clodhoppers, the Babbitts, and the Gantrys of the hinterland. The alienation of city and country ran deep in the 1920s, and took on a regional coloration that was reflected not only in the literature of the decade but in the curious presidential campaigns of 1924 and 1928.

To assay the consequences of the benighted image is even more troublesome than to identify its sources. It provoked a variety of responses in the South. The more defensive southerners developed their own peculiar image of the benighted North, disfigured by slums, overrun by mongrel hordes that sullied the purity of the old Republic, and fatally corrupted by gangsters and their allies. Many editors of the "you're another" school bestirred themselves to toss stink bombs chiefly in the direction of Baltimore. But the pattern was broader than that. In Nashville and New York, Fugitive poets pondered the scene. "Was it possible," they asked, "that

nobody in the South knew how to reply to a vulgar
rhetorician like H. L. Mencken?" Was it not possible
that the southern heritage represented deeper values
than either the boosters of the New South or its facile
critics? And so for a small group of poets and their allies
the trauma of Mencken and Dayton redirected their
thinking toward the viable elements of the southern
tradition, a new consciousness that soon issued in the
Vanderbilt Agrarian movement.

Others rallied to the defense of their native region not
in terms of tradition but in terms of progress. At Vanderbilt, whence the Agrarians held forth, Chancellor
James Kirkland announced that the answer to Dayton
would be the building of new laboratories and Edwin
Mims, head of the English department, hastily assembled a volume on *The Advancing South* that revealed "a
veritable war of liberation" by "constantly enlarging
groups of liberal leaders who are fighting against the
conservatism, the sensitiveness to criticism, the lack of
freedom that have too long impeded Southern progress." In Richmond, Virginius Dabney of the *Times-
Dispatch* compiled in his book, *Liberalism in the South*, the
genealogy of a southern liberal tradition which he
traced back to Thomas Jefferson.

To many thinkers of the progressive school the situation raised the question of problems that called for constructive attention and rational planning. The result was
a burgeoning interest in social science, the establishment
in 1923 of institutes for research in social science at the
Universities of Virginia, North Carolina, and Texas, a
flood of monographs on regional problems from these
and other universities, and ultimately a multitude of

New Deal measures directed to the ills of "the nation's No. 1 economic problem."

Well before the Agrarian and regionalist movements got fully under way a regional literary movement had developed into what was already being called a renaissance before the end of the 1920s. It may be too much to claim, as Oscar Cargill does, that Mencken anticipated the movement and sought to cultivate it in his own backhanded manner. There can be little question, however, that within a few years, "like Aaron's rod Mencken's goad had proved itself a symbol of fertility."

In many respects, then, the image of the benighted South provoked positive reactions in the region: the rediscovery of tradition, the analysis of regional problems, a renaissance in literature, all growing at least in part out of the determination of southerners to erase the deficiencies that had been so widely advertised. On the other hand one is led irresistibly to the conjecture that the image has functioned in some degree as a self-fulfilling prophecy. It established certain presuppositions about what is to be recognized as "typically" southern. It established certain expectations about southern behavior, and its widespread acceptance even in the South vitiated the courage and resolution of southerners who would stand against the savage ideal.

While the image unquestionably has reflected certain elements of southern reality, like all images it blinds the observer to those things that do not fit his mental picture. It has obscured certain important aspects of southern diversity and dynamism behind a pattern of monolithic cussedness. The industrial and urban growth of the twenties, for example; the tremendous

expansion of government services, particularly in highways and public schools; the interracial movement; the
literary renaissance (which merely confirmed the benighted image for those preconditioned to accept it);
the rise of universities and newspapers which inspired
critical analysis of southern problems—none of these
would quite fit into the pattern.

But the image has lived on since the 1920s, reinforced
by a variety of episodes from the Scottsboro trials to the
Oxford riot. That image has not been slain by new
images of traditional agrarianism or the problem South,
nor even by the region's rise from cultural aridity to
literary predominance. In fact, it must be said that the
twentieth-century South has not produced a positive
and viable myth of its own identity powerful enough to
challenge the image of the benighted South.

4

The Central Theme Revisited

In 1928 Ulrich Bonnell Phillips defined the unifying principle of southern history as "a common resolve indomitably maintained" by the white man that the South "shall be and remain a white man's country." "The consciousness of a function in these premises," he said, "whether expressed with the frenzy of a demagogue or maintained with a patrician's quietude, is the cardinal test of a Southerner and the central theme of southern history."

The search for monistic central themes is a quest that has attracted thinkers in all times, and one that seems to have a special fascination for students of the South; but it is also one that has been confounded repeatedly by the diversity of human experience, in the South as well as elsewhere. In its geography and history, in its society and economy, in its politics and ideology, the South has experienced a diversity that resists synthesis under any all-encompassing concept yet found, whether it be in some unfortunate phrase like "sowbelly and segregation" or in the grandiose schemes of romanticism, eco-

59

nomic determinism, or the ideology of white supremacy
—although each of these may throw considerable light
upon the character and history of the South.

At the same time, however, it cannot be denied that
a preoccupation with the issue of race, its mythology
and its symbolism has been one of the major themes of
southern history, with innumerable ramifications into
every aspect of southern life. Every southerner of the
present generation can recognize the continuing validity
of James Weldon Johnson's observation in 1912 that "no
group of Southern white men could get together and
talk for sixty minutes without bringing up the 'race
question.' If a Northern white man happened to be in
the group, the time could be safely cut to thirty minutes."

But to speak of a preoccupation with issues of race is
not to say that there is or ever has been a monolithic
unity in the thought or practice of southern whites on
the subject. For attitudes have ranged from the antislavery Negrophobia of Hinton Rowan Helper to the
liberal equalitarianism of George Washington Cable.
Nor can it be said that either the theory or social reality
of race relations in the South has been constant. They
have, in fact, gone through numerous changes: from
the uncertain status of the first Negroes in early Virginia through the evolution of slavery, from the post-
Revolutionary liberalism to the proslavery argument,
from emancipation and Radical Reconstruction to Redemption and the rise of the twentieth-century system
of white supremacy, and into accelerated change in the
present generation.

Yet, underlying the diversity of southern experience,

certain lines of continuity are apparent. Theory and practice with respect to race relations have moved chiefly in two broad channels developed in the eighteenth and nineteenth centuries. The first of these is what Gunnar Myrdal has labeled the "American Creed." It stems principally from the eighteenth-century philosophy of the rights of man, but has important sources also in Christianity and English law. The ideals "of the essential dignity of the individual human being, of the fundamental equality of all men, and of certain inalienable rights to freedom, justice, and a fair opportunity," says Myrdal, "represent to the American people the essential meaning of the nation's early struggle for independence."

The existence of these ideals, he maintains, has set up a tremendous ideological conflict, which he pictures as largely a psychological struggle within the individual who recognizes that racial prejudices and discriminatory practices do not conform to the generally accepted creed. But in the South, resistance to the "American Creed" has been bolstered by a counter creed which has supplied the white southerner with racial sanctions that are somewhat more than the expression of individual racial prejudice.

If Myrdal's "American Creed" was primarily a product of the struggle for independence, then what Howard W. Odum has called the "credo of the South with reference to the Negro" was in large part the product of sectional conflict. Thrown on the defensive by the vigorous abolitionist assault of the 1830s, the southern leadership perfected an elaborate philosophical justification for the "peculiar institution" of slavery. Whether or not the masses of southern whites were aware of its existence, its influence was pervasive and they accepted most of its basic tenets.

Although the Civil War and Reconstruction shattered the institutional basis upon which race relations had rested in the South for more than two centuries, even this profound upheaval failed to undermine the prevailing patterns of thought on race—proslavery doctrines had penetrated too deeply into southern thinking. During the brief period when President Andrew Johnson was able to leave conservative whites in charge of southern state governments, most of them adopted more or less elaborate "black codes," which sought to retain as much white control over the civil and economic status of Negroes as the new conditions permitted.

As soon as the northern radicals established their dominance, however, the black codes were wiped out. It was now clear that the prevailing southern ideas on race would have to find new modes of social expression. By the time white southern Democrats secured control of their states in the 1870s, new constitutional amendments guaranteed certain rights to Negro citizens. The national Democratic party in 1872 announced its acceptance of these amendments as a *fait accompli*. And while the southern Democrats' rise to power had come about in campaigns characterized by the intimidation of Negroes, those campaigns and the Compromise of 1877 had also been accompanied by Democratic commitments to respect the newly won legal rights of the freedman.

The Democratic Redeemers represented white supremacy, which they believed to be the supremacy of intelligence and character, but they also represented a measure of moderation that did not equate white supremacy as yet with Negro proscription. For a number of years, as C. Vann Woodward has pointed out, certain forces operated as elements of restraint against the triumph of extreme racism. These forces were southern liberalism, a weak thing at best; northern liberalism and the threat of renewed intervention; the conservative spirit of the Redeemers; and the radicalism of the agrarian movement, which for a time united whites and Negroes in their common economic grievances.

With the collapse of these restraints in the 1890s, something endemic in southern thought asserted itself with new vehemence. Because of new circumstances and because of the Reconstruction amendments it found expression in new instrumentalities, but by the first decade of the twentieth century the main patterns of a new "peculiar institution" of white supremacy had become clear. These patterns embodied the now familiar forms of economic subordination, disfranchisement, segregation, and proscription.

One basic aspect of this new peculiar institution, the economic subordination of Negroes under systems of tenancy and wage labor, had never been challenged seriously even by Radical Republicans, whose abundant gifts to enterprise were for the most part distributed to petitioners better organized to push their claims than were the freedmen. Southern whites remained in control of the land and the chief agencies of economic activity, and the labor laws after Reconstruction increasingly reflected the domination of the landowning and merchant classes, sometimes reducing laborers to peonage even with the connivance of the law. Later, with the rise of industry, Negroes found themselves either excluded or limited to the more menial jobs. Even in traditional "Negro jobs" they were faced with the growing competition of white workers. These patterns have remained fairly consistent even into the middle of the twentieth century, with mechanization in agriculture now threatening the Negroes' position in the most traditional of all "Negro jobs."

Other developments were somewhat slower in coming, their evolution stretching out over the generation that followed Reconstruction. Disfranchisement of Negroes was accomplished by the use of fraud and intimidation until such methods became institutionalized in the development of literacy tests and other legal qualifications for the vote and, what was eventually more important, the white primary. The proscription of Negroes from public office was increasingly required until, after the turn of the century, Negroes disappeared entirely from the picture except for a few scattered Republican appointees.

So far the movement constituted a true reaction. Economic subordination, disfranchisement, and political proscription involved a return to conditions roughly approximating those before emancipation. But the keystone of the whole new structure may be found in the caste symbolism of racial segregation. The patterns of segregation were somewhat longer in developing because they represented something rather new. Racial segregation as known in the twentieth century was not a necessary accompaniment of slavery, for that institution in itself provided the necessary symbols and instrumentalities of white supremacy. Segregation as a general civil institution and as a hallowed social myth is essentially a phenomenon of the twentieth century.

When the forces of white supremacy had completed their work, the product was remarkably similar in purpose and appearance to the slave codes of antebellum days, even more complex and thoroughgoing in application, yet different because of new circumstances and especially because of the Reconstruction amendments. If the Negroes' caste status could not be defined legally in terms of slavery or of laws with specific racial discriminations, it could be defined in terms of economic legislation, the establishment of restrictions upon the suffrage, and certain other formal restrictions under the convenient legal doctrine of "separate but equal" facilities, although segregation in practice seldom meant equal facilities and often involved the complete ostracism of Negroes from community activities.

Looking upon their work and finding it good, the authors of the new dispensation saw little need for developing new rationalizations. Rather they found that "numerous theories, already well-worn in the antebellum period, were at hand to justify the caste system." These were the ingrained doctrines of the proslavery argument. The scriptural justification of slavery, for example, reappeared in later years as an argument for discrimination and segregation. The letters column of almost any southern white newspaper revealed citations of the curse called down by the drunken Noah upon his son as evidence that the divine plan ordained the descendants of Ham to be the servants of servants. St. Paul's declaration that God has "made of one blood all nations of men for to dwell on all the face of the earth" is modified, the scriptural segregationist insists, by the additional revelation that He has "determined . . . the bounds of their habitation."

The economic justification of slavery similarly re-emerged in the contention that subordinated Negroes afforded a superior supply of "mudsill" labor. "With all their faults and short-comings," one southerner re-marked, in echo of antebellum sentiments, "there is at least no Anarchist-making material in them." The idea that slavery was a school of civilization was completely transformed after emancipation into the argument that Negroes must now find the opportunity for progress in their own institutions, in the development of their own leadership, even in the development of a separate cul-ture. Thus a contemporary southern governor has de-fended school segregation "in order that we might maintain the older culture of the white race and en-courage the growth of the new and rapidly developing culture of the Negro race . . . through good will and pride in the integrity of our respective racial cultures and way of life."

Some points of the proslavery argument were actually charged with added potency by postwar developments. In a variety of unpremeditated ways, the antebellum web of personal association between whites and Negroes broke down following emancipation. The tenant system disrupted the plantation community; residential segre-gation gradually came to be accepted as the natural pattern in the newer sections of southern towns and cities; a pattern of segregated schools was set by north-ern missionary agencies bent upon supplying the sup-posedly peculiar educational needs of a people newly freed from slavery; and Negroes found opportunities for independence and responsibility in their own separate churches. As the races drew apart and as opportunities for personal acquaintance, even in a paternalistic setting, diminished, the antebellum argument that the Negro was biologically distinct from and inferior to the white man gained an acceptance which had been prohibited during the slavery regime by the opposition of churchmen and by the more intimate knowledge of Negroes. By the end of the nineteenth century a number of writers had carried the argument to its ultimate extreme, in the "Negro a beast" school of thought. While the majority of southern whites had doubtless preferred a more moderate version, which regarded racial differences as simply predisposing the races to different functions in society, there can be little doubt that the biological argument was fundamental to the justification of caste in its changing forms.

Just as the institutional and personal estrangement of the races gave new currency to the biological inferiority argument, so the bitter controversies of the Reconstruction years, which were viewed largely as race conflicts, exacerbated the antebellum assumption of a fundamental antagonism of race. Even Jefferson had been frightened by the potentialities of race conflict if the restraints of slavery should be removed; and the appeal to social stability became one of the most potent weapons in the proslavery arsenal. In like manner, the new peculiar institution, especially its segregation feature, came to be defended as essential "in the interest of orderly government and the maintenance of Caucasian civilization."

White southerners interpreted almost any exercise of the freedmen's new physical and social mobility as a bid for "social equality." The precise meaning of the term was uncertain, but the hypersensitivity of white men to the remotest suggestion of sexual relations between Negro men and white women charged it with overtones of fear. By the 1890s ambitious politicians were playing upon the frustrations generated by the agrarian depression to arouse against the helpless Negroes that old fear of racial conflict which had made rumors of Negro insurrection such a terror to the antebellum countryside.

How simple, then, to seize upon the principle of separation as a means of lessening the possibility of conflict and "amalgamation," at the same time making it a symbol of the Negroes' permanent subordination! Our scanty knowledge of the movement for segregation laws indicates that arguments for their passage emphasized most of all their contribution to public tranquillity. Alfred Holt Stone, of Mississippi, looking back over the early movement for legal separation in 1908, concluded: "In almost every instance of separate car legislation, public sentiment was crystallized into law as the immediate result of intolerable local conditions, not infrequently accompanied by concrete acts of violence." And in subsequent controversies the argument has been advanced time and again that any relaxation of the color line would lead inevitably to incidents and bloodshed. Whether uttered in terms of the potentialities of the situation or in terms of an agitator's threat, the danger of race conflict has been one of the chief justifications for white supremacy in its various forms.

In addition to theories derived from the proslavery argument, there were also certain new factors that could be called into the defense of white supremacy. Out of the sectional conflict there had arisen powerful symbols

of southernism: the romantic picture of the old plantation, the cult of the Confederacy and its heroes, and
especially the memory of Reconstruction. By the turn
of the century the great traumatic experience of Reconstruction was being rehearsed in ever more macabre
terms by politicians, historians, and novelists. It was
probably the novelist Thomas Dixon, Jr., who more
than any other person—aided by Hollywood's all too
faithful translation of one of his books into *The Birth
of a Nation*—fixed the popular view of Reconstruction
as a period of unparalleled horror.

And while the new dispensation was being established, certain new sociological concepts were seized
upon eagerly and incorporated into the rationale of
white supremacy. A new school of sociologists, led by
Franklin H. Giddings, spoke of "innate racial instincts"
and the universal "consciousness of kind," phrases that
found their way into the speeches and writings of southern leaders. Another contribution was William Graham
Sumner's concept of folkways, unchangeable except by
the geological processes of time. This was brought
quickly into play as a support for the new peculiar institution, even for the recently passed segregation laws,
which were rationalized as the ancient folkways of the
South. This idea became perhaps the chief popular support for the way of the South, and had the superior
merit of eliminating the necessity for any moral justification.

In the long run, however, these new supports for the
new peculiar institution were less significant than the
white South's continuing reliance on the proslavery
argument; and even the persistence of the older the-

ories seems less significant than the fact that the white
South so rarely defended its new peculiar institution by
any arguments whatever. "I do not think the [southern
racial attitude] needs any defense," declared Alfred
Holt Stone in 1908. "All it needs is to be understood."

Even during the inflamed decades around the turn of
the century, when the new peculiar institution was being
established, the politicians and publicists who led the
white supremacy campaign relied almost wholly on
irrational appeals to popular emotions and fears long
conditioned by the old proslavery arguments, without
attempting to refurbish these arguments, or even necessarily to repeat them. No sooner was the campaign won,
and segregation and proscription of the Negro firmly
embedded in public policy, than a powerful sentiment
developed to dampen the rekindled fires of racial feeling and to discourage any further public discussion of
race. Politicians who continued to exploit the racial issue
were condemned as demagogues by respectable opinion
in the South as well as in the North.

The white South's reticence in defending its new
peculiar institution can be explained in part by the absence of any effective attack on southern racial practices
remotely comparable to the earlier abolitionist or Radical Republican offensives. Influenced by dynamic forces
of social Darwinism and imperialism, the whole country
was drifting closer to the white South's racial attitudes.
The cult of Anglo-Saxonism, in fact, won its first triumphs in the North before finding a secure repository
in the South—which had sometimes pictured itself as a
Norman chivalry doing battle with the boorish Saxon.
With the increasing respectability of racism and the
growing willingness to let the southern whites handle

the Negro as they saw fit, white southerners felt less need to justify their social system.

What was equally important in the failure to elaborate new justifications was the fact that the new peculiar institution of the South did not provide any convenient ganglion, like the institution of slavery, about which a philosophy of justification could cluster. The new dispensation was not an institution clearly defined in law and in the minds of men, as slavery had been, but rather an ill-defined mélange of diverse factors of economic domination, repression by force and intimidation, political disfranchisement, segregation, and proscription either by private or public imposition. Nor was there any cohesive group like the old slaveholders whose leadership and immediate interests demanded eternal vigilance in the defense of their peculiar institution. The result was that the defense of white supremacy was never fully reformulated, but remained essentially the lengthened shadow of the proslavery argument.

Looking back over the first half of the twentieth century, it becomes clear that a whole series of developments was beginning imperceptibly to undermine the ideological defenses of white supremacy almost as soon as its new institutional patterns became established. The doctrine of biological inferiority was questioned by anthropologists and geneticists who could find no conclusive evidence for it, and their ideas seeped into the public consciousness. Tortured interpretations of the Scriptures were taken less and less seriously by literate southerners. The need for a mudsill labor force was reduced by the development of mechanization in agriculture and industry. The argument for a separate Negro culture ran up against the manifest fact that

Negroes could and did assimilate the general southern
and American patterns, even in their separate institutions. The fear of race conflict with any relaxation of
caste barriers eventually was found to be exaggerated
as Negroes were reenfranchised and segregation was
ruled out in some areas without the predicted blood
bath. And finally, these matters were opened up for
discussion and debate in countless classrooms and organizations.

It would not be feasible within the scope of this essay
to attempt a survey of all the forces and factors in the
twentieth century that have contributed to the erosion
of the ideological defense of white supremacy. C. Vann
Woodward has offered a tentative catalog which includes the following: the NAACP and other national
reform organizations, the Harlem Renaissance, religion
and the social gospel, the American Creed, the Southern Regional Council and similar organizations of
southerners, the migration of Negroes to the North
and into the cities and their subsequent increment of
political influence, a growing prosperity in the South,
the struggles against nazism and communism, and the
rise of the spirit of nationalism since the 1930s.

In times of change it is only natural to look for new
factors as explanations, and most of the above come in
that category. Yet equally important was the traditionally ambiguous nature of the southern position, for it
was this that made the new peculiar institution vulner-
able to the twentieth-century challenges. The spell cast
by the southern credo and the widespread assumption
that it constituted the central explanation of southern

character have obscured the equally fundamental role of its antithesis, which in the larger southernism has been a continuing source of disquietude about the southern credo.

For while the American as southerner has been unable to shake off the proslavery argument, the southerner as American has never abandoned the American Creed. Southern liberals have repeatedly argued that the liberal traditions of American nationalism are to a considerable degree southern in their origins, and national heroes of southern birth like Jefferson and Jackson have been invoked to lend respectability to their views. Even in the period of slavery, white southerners found themselves unable to agree upon, or even fully to accept, the ingenious social theories advanced to justify the original peculiar institution. The biological inferiority argument collided with the Christian view of human personality that white southerners could not help extending to their slaves; and their Jeffersonian liberalism was still too ingrained to permit them to accept the argument for a rigid caste society, rising tier on tier from the mudsill of the happy slave to the planter at the top. "[T]hey never entirely freed their subconscious minds," W. J. Cash has written, "from the old primitive democracy of outlook bequeathed by the frontier."

If few antebellum southerners could really assimilate the neofeudalism of the proslavery argument, fewer still could be found in the New South willing to attack frontally the valuations of the American creed by attempting to build a general theory of society on a mudsill foundation, however implicit the idea may have been in their general outlook. Inhibited by moral taboos,

Gunnar Myrdal has suggested, the southerner has found it impossible to think *"constructively along segregation lines"* or "to think through carefully and in detail how a segregation system could be rationally organized. For *this would imply an open break with the principles of equality and liberty."*

This experience would seem to confirm the observation of Eric Voegelin that "the racial symbolism has comparatively little chance in a society which has gone through an 18th century revolution, because the collective element of racialism is hardly compatible with the belief in the value of the sovereign person and the indestructible soul, and its rights and liberties; and because the biological determinism is incompatible with the idea of reason as a spiritual substance independent of the qualities of the body which houses it."

The force of Voegelin's observation has become apparent in recent decades, during which the South's new peculiar institution has come under severe attack. The changes already brought about by the effects of attack and criticism would seem to necessitate some reexamination of the widely held view largely based upon the history of the nineteenth-century sectional conflict, that "outside" criticism weakens the forces of moderation within the South and generates nothing but intransigence, which in turn generates further criticism and so on into a deepening whirlpool.

Granting some force to this argument, it remains to be recognized that criticism has other effects in a libertarian society, especially when the criticized share many of the assumptions on which the criticism is based. Where those who are free from the pressures of the new peculiar institution have spoken or acted forcefully and judiciously, they have sometimes raised the problem to a level where conscious recognition of basic incongruities becomes inescapable. It is true that psychologists have recognized the possibility of an individual's holding several incompatible views at one and the same time, but Myrdal has suggested that "a need will be felt by the person or group, whose inconsistencies in valuations are publicly exposed, to find a means of reconciling the inconsistencies. This can be accomplished by adjusting one of the conflicting pairs of valuations." Thus criticism of southern racial practice has repeatedly generated temporary intransigence, but in the long run and more significantly it has also compelled self-justification and a slow but steady adjustment by white southerners in the direction of the American faith in equality of opportunity and rights.

This is, in part, evidence of the lasting victory of those earlier critics who wrote the Fourteenth and Fifteenth Amendments into the Constitution. While there have been dire predictions of violence and bloodshed to come from any tampering with southern folkways, there has been a widespread acceptance of Negro suffrage in places where it would have been unthinkable a generation ago. Political leaders, even in the midst of growing tensions (and perhaps because of them), talk increasingly in terms of equal facilities and opportunities. Measures of segregation have generally been defended under the legal fiction of "separate but equal" facilities; and where the attack has come white leaders have generally capitulated to a movement to give at least a semblance of reality to the principle of equality. Whereas in 1940 a Gallup poll showed that about half of the white southerners frankly opposed "equal" education for Negroes, by 1960 even the segregationist leadership avowed equality as its goal and took important steps toward it. This has been a truly profound change in the thinking of white southerners, albeit somewhat obscured in the blood and thunder of newspaper head-lines.

In emphasizing the significance of the American Creed and the pressures brought in its name, I do not intend to say that changes in southern thought and ac-tion have been brought about only by the operation of outside forces, for criticism has also originated in the South. Nor can it be said that the South is a peculiar repository of the eighteenth-century Enlightenment. Other traditional factors have persisted with equal or greater tenacity in the South and have imparted a distinctive flavor to its culture and heritage.

One of the factors has been Christianity. "Conserva-tism in religion," one historian holds, "did not rank far behind traditional racial attitudes as significant causes for the South's retention of its regional distinctiveness." The effect of the social gospel movement has undoubt-edly been a factor in the advanced pronouncements of major southern church bodies on issues of race. Yet the southern churches, on the whole, have remained wedded to orthodoxy in spite of cynical jibes at the "Bi-ble Belt." One result of this has been a deep-seated moral-religious consciousness that has always proved troublesome to the southern credo from the day of primitive antislavery among backwoods Methodists and Baptists to the day of the outstanding practitioner of contemporary evangelism Billy Graham, a native south-erner who has sought and has had unsegregated audi-ences at his meetings in the South.

A consciousness of God's justice and a sense of sin have always been sources of uneasiness among southerners about their peculiar institutions. If Jefferson could tremble when he reflected that God's justice could not sleep forever, or Kate Stone, a Louisiana Episcopalian, could be oppressed with worry about "the moral guilt of it" and "how impossible it must be for an owner of slaves to win his way into Heaven," so white Christians in the New South, according to Bishop Atticus G. Haygood, found themselves "in a state of mental unrest as to their present attitude toward the negroes." Finally, a sense of the importance of the individual, however humble, and his responsibility to the judgment of God have constituted the very core of Christianity, especially in its Protestant expression. These concepts are practically identical with "the belief in the value of the sovereign person and the indestructible soul" described by Eric Voegelin as inhibiting the development of "the collective element of racialism."

The churches have never been the spearhead of social change in the South, it is true. "With all its mighty influence," said Howard Odum, "the power of the church has been in its ideologies and conditioning attitudes and not in its program." But these ideologies and conditioning attitudes have, with few exceptions, functioned as an important restraint upon the most extreme expressions of racism, and have thereby contributed importantly to the erosion of the southern credo.

Not only the church, but also the lingering influence of frontier and agrarian society, have contributed to that "exaggerated individualism" which Cash found to be one of the essential characteristics of the southerner. Respect for the individual personality and a certain easy-going "personalness" in human relations have continued to carry a significance in the South that has not been wholly undermined by the encroachments of industry or urbanism.

A northern visitor to South Louisiana in 1945 discovered that "the habits of both frontier and plantation days are still real along the Mississippi." Among these habits was a sort of institutional kindness that "flows from a thoroughgoing personalness in the aristocratic style of living in the South, and does not exist in the North anywhere." Here was a survival in almost pure form of the patrician attitude of personal affinity between whites and Negroes. Despite the paternalistic and exploitative connotations of this attitude, it has been a source of interracial good will and sometimes of intimate personal contact across the barriers of caste. The kindlier attitudes of antebellum paternalism, surviving among upper-class whites of the New South, gave rise to the tradition that no southern gentleman engages in the harassment of Negroes, but rather regards them with a certain affection and finds a certain affinity of interest with them. He may even take pride in their social and educational progress and attempt to help them in the process, as did J. L. M. Curry of the Peabody Fund and other leaders in the southern education movement.

The neighborly spirit of human relations in the South has democratic as well as aristocratic implications, stemming in some measure from the historical influence of frontier and agrarian democracy that has been as much a part of the southern tradition as the feudal heritage of the plantation. In the southern experience recognition of a community of interest between whites and

Negroes has been manifested by individuals and groups other than those with pretensions to gentility. During any period in southern history since the Civil War some instances of interracial action may be found in the labor movement, among craftsmen, longshoremen, miners, factory workers, and others. In the agrarian revolt of the eighties and nineties the "wool hat boys" found themselves allied with Negro farmers in the struggle against their common economic grievances, and during the 1930s an indigenous organization of tenant farmers and agricultural laborers existed without racial barriers. Middle-class manifestations of a community of interest have appeared in various projects for community improvement such as Community Chest drives.

The older notions of southern gentility and the newer concepts of a community of interest did not expire with the rise of Negrophobia, but on the contrary survived into the twentieth century to give rise to fair-play sentiments and policies. While assuming the inevitability of white supremacy, these movements sought to give Negroes a measure of justice within the system and to keep open the avenues of communication across the barriers. This may be seen in the southern education movement that was developing at the turn of the century, and which inspired even North Carolina's white supremacy leader, Charles Brantley Aycock, to a defense of "the equal right of every child born on earth to have the opportunity 'to burgeon out all that there is within him.'" It may be seen in Edgar Gardner Murphy's conference for the discussion of race problems at Montgomery in 1900. The same spirit motivated the interracial commission established in Atlanta after the riot of 1906, and the South-wide movement of the Com-

mission on Interracial Cooperation, established after
the First World War for "the creation of a better spirit,
the correction of grievances, and the promotion of interracial understanding and sympathy." The chief organizational repository of this tradition (by no means
the only one) since 1944 has been the Southern Regional Council, an interracial group of southerners which
has moved from moderate expressions of fair-play sentiments to outright affirmations of equal rights for all
southerners.

Last of all, the intellectual and economic progress of
Negroes has nurtured the seeds of change by developing Negro institutions and enterprises and professional
occupations, with leaders dependent upon the Negro
community and relatively independent of white control.
Such leadership has frequently provided the spearhead
of the most effective actions against discrimination,
sometimes through tactics of adjustment and at other
times through tactics of protest and criticism.

This indigenous leadership has been of supreme importance and increasing ability, but it has been forced
of necessity to operate in a situation requiring a high
degree of white sympathy and support. One of the most
militant Negro leaders, W. E. B. Du Bois, no less than
Booker T. Washington, long ago recognized that Negro
leadership must address itself ultimately to the better
consciences of white men who, "deeply religious and
intensely democratic . . . feel acutely the false position
in which the Negro problems place them."

A gradual diminution in the force of the southern
credo has now been apparent for several decades.
Though persisting in most of its aspects, the new pecul-

iar institution itself began to show signs of strain under pressure in the thirties; in the forties it began to crack; and in the fifties, its chief symbol and support, Jim Crow, came under virtual sentence of death by the federal courts. The threatened collapse of any institution, however, may bring forth a stubborn defense. Hostile reactions to civil rights programs and especially to the Supreme Court decision in the school segregation cases demonstrated that the old ideas were held with remarkable tenacity. They experienced a certain revival, born in the late 1930s and mounting to a peak of intensity in the 1950s.

This reaction invites comparison with the defense of slavery. The White Citizens' Councils and similar groups, for example, had their counterpart in the vigilance committees of the Old South. Some political spokesmen of the white South revived the dormant antebellum theory of nullification in a new form. Other segregationist leaders—like the secessionists of Charleston, who "adopted as an article of faith the propagation of slavery" with all the zeal of "the Mormons or early Mahometans"—sought to erect the temporary *modus vivendi* of segregation into some kind of eternal moral principle. Analogies of the sort could be pursued at great length, but at several important points the comparison breaks down.

In the first place, the slavery interests of the 1850s were to some extent on the offensive, actively seeking the extension of slavery into the territories. The tone of the 1950s reaction was decidedly defensive, seeking only to hold the ground already occupied, or even to retreat to the line of separate but equal.

In the second place, the oratory and literature of the

later reaction showed no serious promise of developing
a positive philosophical justification of the new peculiar
institution. An intellectual leadership of the sort that
perfected the proslavery argument was conspicuous by
its absence. Such efforts at rationalization as appeared
leaned heavily upon charging the opposition with ques-
tionable motives and susceptibility to insidious influences. This observation may seem to place an excessive
emphasis upon the rationality of human motivation in
an area where irrationality has often ruled. Yet the lack
of a reasoned defense may very well have constituted
the serious long-range vulnerability of an institution in
conflict with so many values deeply imbedded in the
traditions and thought of the people.

In the third place, the solid front of southern whites
in the 1850s had been splintered by the 1950s. What
George Washington Cable once called the "Silent South"
was by then articulate. Church organizations, citizens'
groups, individuals, even prominent political leaders
demonstrated publicly their indifference or hostility to
the old southern credo. Assertion of the American
Creed in the face of serious pressures makes it difficult
to assume that the old spell of unanimity will ever be
revived. Even spokesmen for the new reaction seem in
many cases to have adopted in private the attitude,
which sometimes crops out in public utterances, that
their function is in the nature of a rear guard delaying
action rather than a lasting revival of white supremacy
doctrines.

Adequate appraisal of contemporary developments is
an uncertain business. But one southern historian has
been "so bold as to maintain that recent changes are of

sufficient depth and impact as to define the end of an era of Southern history." If the dynamics of recent events can inspire so bold an observation, they must also lead us to consider whether we may be witnessing the disappearance of the South as a conscious entity.

For if we accept the analysis of U. B. Phillips, that day when white supremacy should be no longer the cardinal tenet and primary aim of white southerners would be the day in which the South would become but another geographical part of the United States, for the central theme of its history and the chief source of its unity would have come to an end. It would be a rash prophet indeed who would forecast when that day might come, but in view of general trends over recent decades and the direction of public policy today, it can no longer seem so completely outside the range of possibility as it must have seemed to Phillips in 1928.

But would a decline and fall of white supremacy necessarily reduce the South to merely another geographical part of the United States? Only if we must accept the dictum of Phillips that white supremacy is the central and indispensable determinant of southern peculiarity. Though for a century and a half the issue of race has been an important key to southern character and one of the chief issues on which other elements of southernism and Americanism have interacted, we cannot in the light of recent events continue to regard it as an immutable feature of southern life.

Present perspectives suggest, indeed, that the "credo of the South with reference to the Negro" can no longer be regarded as the indispensable key to southern distinctiveness—just as, for that matter, the American Creed fails to explain fully the broader national character. The southern credo has never summarized the diverse aspects of the southern heritage. This is recognized in popular thought, for popular stereotypes of the southerner have flourished and have been readily recognized without any overt reference to the issue of race. Southerners themselves have time and again manifested intense regional loyalties in situations dissociated from an emphasis on the issue of race—the cotton mill campaign of the 1880s, for example, the southern education movement around the turn of the century, the campaign against freight rate discrimination, the Agrarian manifesto of 1930, and the development of an academic ideology of southern regionalism by Howard W. Odum and his disciples.

The historian can report, too, that the Negro has been a southerner. The point is seldom comprehended in the general usage of the term *southerner*, but the records and literature of the South bear voluminous recognition of the fact. In making the culture of the South, W. J. Cash asserted, "Negro entered into white man as profoundly as white man entered into Negro—subtly influencing every gesture, every word, every emotion and idea, every attitude." In shaping patterns of speech, of folklore, of music, of literature, and in the manifold products of their labor, Negro southerners have everlastingly influenced and enriched the culture of their region. To overlook this contribution would be to neglect much that has made the South distinctive.

The Negro has been a southerner. The Negro, too, has been an American. In the promises of the American Creed, rather than in programs of escape or revolution, he has found the fundamental key to his aspirations.

According to a Negro Georgian, "Negroes are really more American than most whites. Actually they are more loyal. Negroes are trying to achieve their full status as American citizens. . . . This fight forces Negroes to be nationalistic."

In the perspective of the southerner as American, then, we may gain insight into the Negro southerner as well as the white. The Negro southerner, like the white, has been moving on the momentum of slavery but also on the momentum of the American Creed. Starting with tremendous handicaps from slavery—social, economic, psychological, and intellectual—his patterns of adjustment to the situation have sometimes been modeled after the patterns of slavery, in the submissiveness of the old time "darky" or even in the limited progressivism of Booker T. Washington's "Atlanta Compromise." But at the same time there have been other patterns of southernism and of more militant striving after the promises of the American Creed.

Finally, we return to Phillips' central theme of southern history. To recognize the Negro as a southerner is perhaps to deliver the *coup de grâce* to the Phillips thesis, but before abandoning it precipitately, we must render a proper deference to its great validity in explaining much about the South. Phillips' essay dealt chiefly with the antebellum South and in that context it emphasized the importance of slavery, as a race issue, in forging that consciousness of southern unity which culminated in secession and the Confederacy. It was reprinted, most appropriately, at the end of a volume entitled *The Course of the South to Secession*. At the time of Phillips' writing it was an interpretation that was losing favor in many quarters, but more recent historians like Allan Nevins and Arthur M. Schlesinger, Jr., have tended to turn back to slavery and racism as the fundamental issue in their explanations of the sectional controversy and the Civil War.

In this essay, however, we have tried to view the subject in a broader context than politics, which Phillips scarcely did, and also in the perspective of a New South now older than the Old South ever was while it existed. In this perspective a larger southernism is an unquestionable reality, especially to those who have grown up in the South, and the historian can list some of the objective factors that produced it: a distinctive historical experience involving defeat and poverty; the climate and physical setting with their effects on life, tempo, emotion, and character; the presence of the Negro and his pervasive influence on the whole life of the region; the powerful religious heritage and the knowledge of good and evil; and finally, the persistence of an essentially rural culture with its neighborliness in human relations.

Yet the historian who is also a southerner knows that the reality of southernism—like so many important aspects of experience—defies precise definition or objective analysis. This reality he knows best as a southerner, for whom it is a subjective experience of land and people and ways of living, which has become a ground for attachment and loyalty. As an historian he can only report that the many different kinds of people living in the South's many widely different parts find a large degree of common meaning in their infinitely various personal experiences.

He can report, in short, that the southern way of life
has involved infinitely more than a system of segregation and proscription. And more and more frequently,
as time passes, he can report that a consciousness of
loyalty to the South may even take the form of opposition to the old southern credo. More than one white
southerner has experienced the same change that came
into the life of Katherine DuPre Lumpkin, who, after
abandoning her native heritage of racial beliefs and
practices, was "haunted by the old dogma, that but one
way was Southern, and hence there could be but one
kind of Southerner." "I could still half believe this," she
said, "even as late as the 1920's, perhaps partially remain under the spell of its old authority. . . . But then
I learned that this was not so. It could not be. What had
altered me was the South's own doing. The beginning of
the beginning for my change lay far back in our history."

5

Howard W. Odum:
A Preliminary Estimate

"Howard W. Odum was the Eli Whitney of the Modern South," said the Washington *Post* shortly after his death in 1954. "He inspired a revolution. Certainly there was no one—unless it was Franklin Roosevelt—whose influence was greater than Odum's on the development of the region below the Potomac."

Whatever the future estimate of Howard Odum's significance, historians of the South delving into the first half of the twentieth century will increasingly encounter his name. They will find it useful to come to grips with his theory and method of regionalism, and they will find in his voluminous publications and papers a tremendous store of both primary and secondary materials for the history of the South. The papers now deposited in the Southern Historical Collection at Chapel Hill constitute one of the finest individual manuscript collections relating to the first half of the century. A scanning of these papers shows them to be rich in materials on every aspect of southern life and development.

Howard Odum was a man of unusual vitality, active

not only as a creative scholar in his own right but as an organizer and administrator of scholarship and, what is more, persistently active in many aspects of public affairs. For these reasons, it is pertinent at this point to commence some evaluation of his work and to emphasize the value for historians both of his work and of the materials he left behind.

Born near Bethlehem, Georgia, May 24, 1884, Howard Odum lived on the farm until his family moved when he was thirteen to Oxford, Georgia. Graduated from Emory College in 1904, Odum taught school for a short while in the rural community of Toccopola, Mississippi. From here, the story still has it at the nearby University of Mississippi, he commuted to classes on muleback and took an M.A. in the classics in 1906. During this period he was already developing the interest in Negro life and folklore that was to occupy much of his time in the future, seeking out "music physicianers" and gathering Negro folksongs and folklore, particularly in the neighborhood of his Georgia and Mississippi homes. It was Thomas Pierce Bailey of the University of Mississippi, himself already busy with studies of Negro life and race relations, who turned Odum toward the relatively new field of social science and sent him off to Clark University, where he took a Ph.D. in psychology under G. Stanley Hall in 1909, followed by another in sociology at Columbia University under Franklin H. Giddings in 1910.

His Columbia dissertation, published in 1910 as *Social and Mental Traits of the Negro*, was to be the first in a long series of works depicting the folk life of the South. It was an effort at an objective view of the life of the great masses of Negroes, seeking "to reach some insight into what the Negro appears to be and what he may possibly become in his future development." It is on the whole a grim and discouraging picture of Negro shortcomings. But it is packed with detailed facts gathered from personal observations as well as available sources, and for that reason has considerable usefulness for the social historian. It should be read with caution, however, and will perhaps appear to the contemporary reader as significant primarily in presenting the best "respectable" thought of the white man on the subject during a period when racialism still dominated the intellectual world and disfranchisement and segregation were reaching a climax. There were only the most rudimentary suggestions of the distinction between cultural and racial traits that would later become commonplace. Whatever the sources of his differences, which Odum did not specifically define, the Negro was different from the white man and would have to seek his destiny in his own separate culture.

While Odum never specifically repudiated this first volume in the light of changing currents in anthropological and sociological thought (and there was much that did not need to be repudiated), he demonstrated in other ways a capacity for growth and change. Active in the affairs of the Commission on Interracial Cooperation from the time of its founding in 1919, he progressed from its approach of winning gains for Negro southerners within the context of segregation to a considerably more advanced position as president of the successor organization, the Southern Regional Council. In response to an appeal from John Temple Graves in 1944 that he endorse the principle of Negro advancement within the framework of segregation, Odum inquired: "From the scientific viewpoint, as well as from the viewpoint of American democracy and the stated principles of Christianity is it possible to commit a whole people 'forever' to a principle which violates these main tenets?" So far had Odum moved since his first scholarly effort in 1910.

Other early products of his interest in Negro folk life were not so subject to the vicissitudes of time. In 1909 and 1911 he published in two lengthy articles the fruits of his collecting expeditions in Mississippi and Georgia: "Religious Folk-Songs of the Southern Negroes," and "Folk-Song and Folk-Poetry as Found in the Secular Songs of the Southern Negroes." The former was his dissertation of 1909, the first two sentences of which set forth a view of folk sociology that was to characterize his work over the years: "To know the soul of a people and to find the source from which flows the expression of folk-thought is to comprehend in a large measure the capabilities of that people. To obtain the truest expression of the folk-mind and feeling is to reveal much of the inner consciousness of a race."

After leaving Columbia, Odum went to a position with the Philadelphia Bureau of Municipal Research, for which he made a study of Negroes in the public schools of the city. In 1912 he went to the University of Georgia, where he rose to the positions of professor of educational sociology and director of the summer school. Then he moved briefly to Emory as professor of sociology and dean of liberal arts. There he aided in Emory's move to Atlanta and also participated in some of the early developments in the organization of the Commission on Interracial Cooperation.

After one year at Emory, he made his last permanent

move, to the University of North Carolina, in 1920.
Harry W. Chase, the new president of the university,
had known Odum as a contemporary at Clark University, and for some time had been interested in bringing
him to Chapel Hill as part of an imaginative program
for building the university. Winning authorization for a
school of public welfare from the board of trustees early
in the year, President Chase secured the election of Dr.
Odum in February.

Before leaving Atlanta, Odum plunged with characteristic vigor into the organization of his program. As a
beginning, he took up the organization of two summer
institutes for public welfare: one for county superin-
tendents of public welfare, the other for social and welfare workers, especially Red Cross workers. Odum had
been connected with Red Cross work during World
War I; he obtained the assistance of the Red Cross in
setting up the two summer institutes and later a substantial grant from the Red Cross to aid the university
in establishing its School of Public Welfare and a sociology department in the fall of 1920.

Throughout the first year and for some years to come,
Professor Odum was constantly on the go about the
state, speaking and making acquaintances, promoting
his school of public welfare and his summer institutes.
From these early beginnings he moved soon to other
successes—the establishment in November, 1922, of the
Journal of Social Forces and, with a grant from the Laura
Spelman Rockefeller Memorial Foundation, the establishment in 1924 of the Institute for Research in Social
Science, the first university institute of its kind in the
country.

From the beginning *Social Forces* drew the respect of sociologists all over the country and even the qualified approbation of Baltimore's hatchet man, H. L. Mencken, who read one of the early issues from cover to cover, "perhaps a sufficient tribute to its interest from a man who shares the common journalistic prejudice against the uplift in all its forms." He found "rather too much glow and eloquence and too little practical information" in the early issue, but saw promise of field work and factual investigation into a region whose "problems have been discussed endlessly, but never investigated." Over the years *Social Forces* was to grow from an organ of progressive uplit into a more scientific journal of sociology, and from a somewhat provincial organ very quickly into a journal of national significance.

The Institute for Research in Social Science was likewise increasingly productive, with studies of regional history and problems in race relations, economics, mill villages, penology, and other matters. Researches carried on through the institute kept a flow of articles moving into *Social Forces*, and by the end of the school year 1929–1930 had resulted in thirty-three published books and monographs, twenty-three of which were published through the University of North Carolina Press. At the same time it served to build up the personnel and prestige of the sociology department and to develop the graduate school by providing a number of assistantships. It soon attracted attention to Chapel Hill throughout the region as "the Wisconsin of the South," and quickened interest in the study and analysis of southern economic and social problems.

Looking back on the early years, it seems in retrospect

that Odum was moving from one triumph to another. President Chase credited him in 1927 with having "built from nothing in seven years a department that has made the University internationally known in this field." But looking back two decades later, Odum recalled that "when we started the Department of Sociology we were so unpopular, had no students, and were generally rated to be canceled off. We had to take our old doctrine of letting emergencies make us do something better than we would have without the emergency, that is, we established *Social Forces* and the Institute for Research in Social Science because we had time and the University was not quite ready or willing for us to do the other thing."

Not only the ignorance and suspicion of a new discipline, but overt hostility in some quarters plagued the early years of Odum's program. He early encountered the fanatical currents of the 1920s when David Clark, editor of the *Southern Textile Bulletin* in Charlotte, found among the contributors to *Social Forces* in 1923 the names of Homer Folks and Owen R. Lovejoy, "parasites who have for years been professional agitators," Miss Grace Abbott, "well known as a tricky and underhand manipulator of statistics," and Frank Tannenbaum, "an ex-convict and confessed Red," and complained that the university "was never intended as a breeding place for socialism and communism."

In the great war between evolution and fundamentalism, the *Journal of Social Forces* became the object of attack from clerical sources. Two articles in the January, 1925, issue, by Harry Elmer Barnes and L. L. Bernard, were singled out as having brought Bible Christianity into question. Bitter protests issuing from ministerial associations in Charlotte and Gastonia inspired similar protests all over the state and the advertisement of petitions inquiring whether the state paid any support toward the *Journal of Social Forces*—seeking facts, Odum said, which could have been determined in five minutes by application to the editors of the journal. "It is rather startling," the Methodist Odum wrote to the leader of one of these groups, "to be devoutly working for a greater southern Christianity, to find one's self at break-o'-day a sort of outcast in the minds of a group which I have believed in and stood by all my life."

President Chase stood firm, as he had against efforts to outlaw the teaching of evolution, and in an eloquent address to the students at the opening of the academic year in September, 1925, he defended the right of the university to freedom of inquiry and thought. The legislature in the following year killed a bill designed to strike at any expression of religious unorthodoxy in state institutions.

Again in 1926 Odum was to be faced with serious misunderstanding of his purposes. With the cooperation of the School of Commerce, he proposed to the executive committee of the North Carolina Cotton Manufacturers' Association an investigation to determine the causes of the high and expensive labor turnover in the cotton mills. The mere sight of Odum, wrote a former colleague, Gerald W. Johnson, "drove the North Carolina textile manufacturers into spasms of terror." The "benevolent doctor" had thought to confer a favor. "When, instead of falling on his neck, they covered their faces, shrieked and fled, he stood dumfounded and then withdrew from the field in wonder and amazement." In an industry "swayed by such incoherent, unreasoning fear," thought Johnson, it was not surprising that there was such a lack of statistical information on other matters, such as style trends, that the industry "fights along blindly and inevitably plunges into pitfalls that might be avoided easily if common sense ruled it more and panic less frequently."

The misunderstandings and criticisms of Odum's program were to continue throughout his life, reaching perhaps their peak in 1941 when his magnum opus, *Southern Regions*, was banned from the elementary and high schools of his native state by Eugene Talmadge's state school board. But already as early as 1928 Odum had so successfully weathered the attacks on his program that he could relax in the philosophical view that "there is this fine thing about North Carolina that she interprets democracy to mean that anybody can say anything he wants to about anybody else, but North Carolina has not in the past taken action upon her citizens"; whereas "the tendency in Georgia and Mississippi is not only to *say* things but to *do* things, making it impossible for an individual of independence to work in freedom." His tendency, then, was "not to give too much importance to Clark's comment."

Meanwhile, despite the pressure of administrative duties and tensions created by outside attacks, he was getting back to the creative work that was his first love. After fifteen years without a volume there suddenly appeared three in 1925. One dealt with the general problems of a public welfare program. This was *Systems of Public Welfare*, written and edited with D. W. Willard. Turning to the challenge of organized research into regional problems that was presented by the Institute for Research in Social Science, Odum compiled and

edited a symposium on *Southern Pioneers in Social Interpretation*, emphasizing the development of a southern
tradition of social analysis and reform, and seeking out
the "Southern Promise" in that approach.

Briefly, then, he returned to his original interest, and
with Guy B. Johnson edited a compendium of Negro
songs, *The Negro and His Songs*, to be followed the next
year by *Negro Workaday Songs*. Within a few more years
the materials from many years of compiling Negro folklore were to be charged with creative artistry in the almost poetic trilogy of a wandering "Black Ulysses," a
figure inspired by a Negro folk character known as Left-
Wing Gordon, who had been found by Odum in a crew
of highway workmen. The three small volumes, *Rainbow
Round My Shoulder*, *Wings on My Feet*, and *Cold Blue
Moon*, caught as no academic study or compendium
could the spirit of the Negro folklore that had occupied
Odum's attention over the years.

But this man of complex and multiple interests was
still busy with general sociology and with public affairs.
In 1927 he published a text, *Man's Quest for Social Guid-
ance*. With Katharine Jocher he wrote in 1929 *An Intro-
duction to Social Research*. Meanwhile he edited a social
study series for the University of North Carolina Press
and the American Social Science Series for Henry Holt.
In 1930 he was called upon by President Hoover to set
up the program of social research that finally led to the
publication three years later of the monumental compendium, *Recent Social Trends in the United States*. Although the research was directed by William F. Ogburn,
Odum actually organized the project, secured Rockefeller Foundation support, and served as assistant director of research. In 1930 he made a study of the penal

system of North Carolina that resulted in ultimate reforms, and within a few years was serving in multiple
capacities as adviser and board member of a number of
New Deal agencies in North Carolina.

After 1930 Odum's work reached its most mature expression in his explorations of the southern regions and
in the development of his theory and methodology of
regionalism. His previous career had pointed to this
culmination. Regionalism was a natural outgrowth of
the whole direction of his work through *Social Forces*,
the Institute for Research in Social Science, his welfare
work, and the studies of Negro folklore. It was also an
outgrowth of the work on *Recent Social Trends*, which
sought to inventory the social resources and trends of
the nation much as Odum was soon to do in greater
detail for the southern regions. Already Odum's colleague, Rupert Vance, had commenced his inventories
of the South. All of this blended with the brew of regionalism that had begun to ferment in the 1920s. For
a decade regionalism had occupied the pages of literary
journals and had been implicit in the publication of
"little magazines" of regional import both in the South
and elsewhere; it became the subject of discussion
among geographers, anthropologists, economists, political scientists, and sociologists; it was attracting a more
technical consideration under the heading of "regional
planning," although this usually meant metropolitan
planning at first. The idea was soon to receive increased
emphasis both as a theoretical and administrative approach under the New Deal administration.

In 1930 southern regionalism burgeoned in two quite
different volumes representative of conflicting approaches that were to agitate the remainder of the dec-

ade. One was the Vanderbilt Agrarian manifesto, *I'll Take My Stand*, an eloquent and artistic appeal for the rural virtues. Odum credited the book with some value, but as he wrote his friend in Baltimore, it did not recognize "that all of the old southern romanticism has been thoroughly interwoven with a realism, which, even though in the long run may develop a fine culture, is at the present a pretty sordid fact. . . . What we have to find now is the product of what was and what is—as a fact and not as an ideal."

This is what Odum sought to do in the nearest thing to an historical work that ever came from his typewriter, *An American Epoch: Southern Portraiture in the National Picture*, the subtitle of which foreshadows the central theme of his more mature regionalism. *An American Epoch* was the product of a creative insight much like that of Wilbur J. Cash, which presented the realities of folk life in the New South with a vividness that no formal historial could hope to achieve. Through two semifictional characters, "Uncle John" and "the old Major," and their numerous progeny, Odum presented an impressionistic view of the evolution of southern folk through four generations. Displaying constant irritation at the prejudices and petty sensitivity of many southerners, he was no less disturbed at the frequent insensitivity of northern observers to southern realities. Critical of the South's shortcomings, it was nonetheless a hopeful book, looking for "a colorful picture of an achieving region rather than a pale print of the sensitive South."

It was in this spirit that Odum approached his supreme opportunity when the General Education Board in the autumn of 1931 made a grant to the Social Science Research Council for a southern regional study that was to run for three years. The following year the program was set up with a committee chaired by Benjamin B. Kendrick and under the general direction of Howard Odum. That same year, 1932, saw the posthumous publication of Frederick Jackson Turner's *The Significance of Sections in American History*. In this work Turner had prepared an important historical foundation for the structure of regionalism that Odum was about to erect. With the frontier gone as an active force in American history, Turner, historian of the frontier, cast about for some other unifying concept that would help explain the new nation coming into being. He found it in the development of sectionalism, which seemed to him a permanent characteristic of the American scene, firmly based on historical experience and on differing interests that could be projected into the future. The United States had become a congeries of sections which in their extent, and to a degree in their relations, bore a distinct resemblance to the European nations. Much of the legislation of Congress, from the multiplicity of sectional interests that played upon its drafting, resembled treaties negotiated between sovereign nations.

While sectionalism, as conceived by Turner, was a manifestly valid approach to American history, and while it laid a foundation in history for the regionalism that Odum was conceiving, it did not for Odum provide the method of achieving the potentialities of American life. Sectionalism he considered the source of infinite evil. It abounded in conflict. It drew off into controversy talent and energy that should be expended in the rational study and development of society. *Regionalism* was

the word that would exorcise the evil spirits of sectionalism. Regionalism would seek to ameliorate conflict. It
would seek the integration of the region into the nation,
recognizing differences and encouraging diversity but
only in the 'context of the general national welfare.
America, the whole, was greater and more important
than any of its parts.

This difference, which represented a part of his disagreement with the Vanderbilt Agrarians, was to become for Odum one of the fundamental tenets, if not
the central theme, of his new regionalism. Sectionalism
was the *bête noire*, the enemy at which Odum hammered
for the rest of his life. It was a protean monster, appearing now in the form of an attack upon a president's wife
for entertaining the wife of a Negro congressman, now
in the form of a northern committee rushing to investigate the actions of Governor Talmadge, again in a
Dixiecrat revolt, or again in a New England governor
advising manufacturers to raise money to unionize
southern labor as a protective device. Time and again,
through people both North and South, Odum was active in the effort to discourage movements that he
thought tended to arouse sectional passions.

This approach of discouraging controversy, followed
by Odum with a rare consistency, was soon paradoxically to be the occasion for a tempestuous disagreement
within the southern regional project, a disagreement
that seemed to many of Odum's colleagues a mere tem-
pest in a semantic teapot, but which to him was a matter
of essentials. The flare-up, set off by an article by Benjamin B. Kendrick in the *Southwest Review*, resulted in
serious disagreement, but it also had the merit of sharp-

ening Odum's expression of the difference between "sectionalism" and "regionalism." Odum was disturbed not only by this article, but also by a general trend toward the revival of sectional feeling. "What is happening in many cases," he wrote to George Fort Milton, "and particularly in the South, especially in North Carolina and other places, is a resurgence of the 'old sectionalism' rationalized as regionalism. This distinction is not merely academic. . . . What is happening is a revivification of Turner's sectionalism."

In reaction to the situation, Odum dictated a memorandum setting forth his "rather positive dissent from the Committee's apparent position." In revised form the memorandum later appeared in *Social Forces* and in *Southern Regions*. One of the reverberations set off by the disagreement was a letter from Donald Davidson of the Vanderbilt Agrarian group to John D. Wade of Georgia that came indirectly to Odum's hands. It contains one of the most trenchant criticisms of Odum's approach to come from any source and bespeaks a realism not always attributed to the Agrarians. "Odum," said Davidson, "I am sure, must realize that pure politics, pure science, pure art never remain pure very long. Politics runs into economic considerations, and economics finally runs into politics. Odum will not escape the political aspects of Southern economic and cultural problems simply by insisting that he has a regional, not a sectional, program." What, Davidson asked, if the Tennessee Valley Authority should put that area into competition with Grand Rapids, producing furniture more cheaply with cheaper electric power? "They will then go to Congress, or to some appropriate bureau, and raise all the devil they can with Odum's regionalism. I can't see the difference in the end. The bricks will fly, for one reason or another. Our business is to dodge them, and maybe toss a brick in return, now and then." The distinction that Odum was seeking to make might be useful for purposes of study, but "sectionalism offers the political approach, which is the natural approach that our history and governmental habits invite."

Regionalism is more than an attack upon sectionalism, of course. A concept with important implications in literature, geography, history, ecology, anthropology, psychology, economics, political science, and sociology, it is too complicated in all of its richness to unravel here. In Odum's *Southern Regions of the United States* and more explicitly in his *American Regionalism*, written with Harry E. Moore, these multiple implications are brought forward. Regionalism is a means of synthesis of all the social sciences and, to some extent, of the humanities. It is the method whereby one can study society and see it whole, not in bits and snatches from the viewpoint of some narrow specialty. Yet, it is more than that. It is a program of action. It is an approach whereby the regions may be integrated into the national whole without losing their differentiation. It is a practical basis on which to pursue social planning. It is all of these things and more, but it is not any one of them. Regionalism is a grandiose concept that must be grasped whole or not at all, else it degenerates into a kind of "sectional-local" provincialism.

Whatever the value of the insights into objective reality here, Odum had a new vision of the potentialities of regionalism. That sectionalism is a real force in American society, no contemporary can deny. Whether regionalism still has potentialities beyond the study and description of society, perhaps only the future can tell. But Odum never contented himself with regionalism as a purely academic discipline. Odum, said two of his colleagues, Rupert Vance and Katherine Jocher, "never concealed the fact that he was a sociologist and that certain social theories implied certain appropriate social action." Regionalism provided the method whereby human intelligence could be used most effectively in the solution of social problems.

Practical application of the concepts and programs set forth in *Southern Regions* would require the establishment of some kind of organized research and planning. Shortly after the publication of that volume, the General Education Board sponsored a ten-day Institute on Southern Regional Development and the Social Sciences at Chapel Hill, in June, 1936, to consider the implications of the findings in *Southern Regions* and to look into the problems of actual planning in certain fields of regional economy and culture. Out of the meeting there came a committee, Howard Odum, chairman, to work out the ways and means of establishing a coordinated program of research and planning for developing and carrying into effect programs for regional improvement.

In Odum's mind implementation of this program gradually took form as a Council on Southern Regional Development, a private and independent agency to be financed by support from individuals and foundations. The council would operate in four general fields: race relations, land tenure and farm relations, economics and labor relations, and public relations and administration. A conference of leading businessmen, educators, labor leaders, and other public figures, assembled by Odum's committee in Atlanta, endorsed the program in January, 1938. The Commission on Interracial Cooperation, of which Odum was now president, agreed in February to merge with the new group. Odum confidently proposed a twelve-year program with a budget of at least two million dollars, most of which he expected to obtain from the major foundations.

The Council on Southern Regional Development, had it materialized, would have been the crowning achievement of Odum's regionalism. It was very nearly accomplished. Odum got endorsements from hundreds of prominent citizens, both inside the South and out. He had, if not promises, at least tentative assurances of support from the General Education Board, the Rosenwald Fund, and the Rockefeller Foundation. He spoke of some man of public affairs, like Owen D. Young or Arthur Page, to head up the group, and definitely planned that Will W. Alexander should come back South from his government work to serve as an executive.

But the program ran afoul of dangerous and confusing crosscurrents in the late thirties. The resurgence of sectionalism that Odum had feared, and that he continued to fight, was already making it difficult for the social scientist who wanted to approach regional problems in a dispassionate manner. It was the year of the National Emergency Council's *Report on Economic Conditions of the South* with its ill-fated phrase, "the Nation's No. 1 economic problem," which was seized upon so eagerly by controversialists bent upon plunging the South once again into a sectional dither. It was also the year of the presidential "purge," the wage and hour law,

and other events that carried sectional overtones. But in
the end it was the activities of other liberal-minded people that did more to frustrate Odum than the resurgent
sectionalism, which after all might have been channeled
into a program for regional development.

The trouble was in the multiplicity of organizations
pointing the same way. By August, 1938, Odum was
beginning to despair of his council plan, "because there
are so many diversified groups in the South," he wrote
the chairman of the Southern States Industrial Council,
"each one bent on doing the whole job in its own way."
"Between the Right Honorable FD," he wrote to another
friend the same day, "the Southern Conference for
Human Welfare, and twenty other groups that are literally taking the lead to do what the Council ought to do,
I think I'll presently go heat-wave hay-wire!!!"

The Southern Conference for Human Welfare
seemed briefly to offer some remote possibility of an
agency through which Odum's aspirations might be
achieved, but he had decided before its first meeting in
November, 1938, that his old friend Wilson Gee was
correct when he predicted that it would probably follow
a course similar to that of the old Southern Sociological
Congress: "It will stir up a great deal of enthusiasm and
do some good work over a period of a few years and
then, as is true of so many organizations of that nature,
it will likely dwindle and pass off the stage." In the end
Odum decided not to go to the meeting in Birmingham.
He concluded that "the whole thing was initiated from
a communistic source." The effect, even the purpose, of
the conferences, he later concluded, was to split the
South, which sometimes seemed to Odum incapable of

coming to agreement with itself. Odum's general approach to practical issues can perhaps best be illustrated by his report on a talk with Frank P. Graham, who had been chosen president of the conference:

> I pointed out that it was my opinion that he would have none of the universities in the South, he would not have the state conferences of social work, nor the general education forces, and of course none of the business men: and that, after all, strategy is of the essence of principle. It seems to me [that] to set the South in a sectional strife and the nation in a program of labeling of those who do not follow any ideology that comes up is a most unfortunate strategy.
>
> . . . .
>
> It seems most unfortunate that we have to be labeled and purged because of the immaturity of approach which seems hellbent to make the South show up its emotional and provincial qualities.

Nevertheless, Odum decided to continue with his program independent of the Southern Conference, as Graham had suggested. Soon, however, other groups appeared. The Tennessee Valley Authority began to plan a council composed of representatives from the universities and land-grant colleges. Odum thought momentarily that he might combine forces with this group, but he later withdrew his suggestions. In December, 1939, the Southern Governors' Conference set forth a ten-year program that Odum thought was lifted from his council plans. All of these programs proved to be merely transitory arrangements, mere conference ideas, as against what Odum had planned—an enduring agency "authoritatively representative" of the region and well supported. But for the present, Odum wrote Will Alexander, they would have to continue as for the last fifteen to twenty years, "cheerfully but stubbornly, using a punting game, and develop good teams and strategy."

The council that Odum envisioned never developed. He continued to think about it and plan for it while the South as a whole moved further along the path of resurgent sectionalism, fighting for the equalization of freight rates, seeking defense and war industries, arguing the issue of race relations that began during World War II to take on a new complexion as a dispute over segregation itself. The correspondence of Odum as chairman of the Commission on Interracial Cooperation presents a clear picture of the shift in emphasis to this issue by Negro leaders especially, and some whites. Odum now turned his main attention to the new problems that were developing with the war, organizing research for defense purposes; and through his connections in the South, he gathered a formidable collection of materials on racial tensions that was organized and analyzed in *Race and Rumors of Race*, a volume to which historians will be indebted for insights into the thinking of both whites and Negroes during that period.

In 1943 the race issue presented itself in a form that offered another opportunity for the establishment of a regional council. When a group of Negroes gathered in Durham, North Carolina, to challenge the white people of the South who believed in equal opportunity to offer the Negro a "New Deal," Odum took the lead in organizing a conference of whites in Atlanta, consisting largely of people associated with the interracial commission. Out of these meetings came a joint meeting in

Richmond which organized the Southern Regional Council, a group ostensibly designed to grow into a general council for regional development. But not so. In retrospect now, the Southern Regional Council seems but a reorganization of the old Commission on Interracial Cooperation, with Odum continuing as president, and there is reason to believe that Odum saw it realistically as nothing more than that. Its inspiration lay in the new racial problems created by the war, or at least exacerbated by the war. Its early policy meetings were dominated by the segregation issue, on which the council during its early years did not take a definite stand. Until about the end of the war Odum still had hopes that the council might grow into the more general regional-development organization that he wanted to see, but he finally concluded, as he wrote to the executive director, Guy B. Johnson, the plain fact was "that I have not been able to deliver the goods in so far as getting the thing integrated and not conflicting with other groups."

After this, Odum's later career was taken up mostly with his research and writing. Another volume of folk portraiture, *The Way of the South*, carried *An American Epoch* forward through another generation. Then came two volumes on general sociology, *Understanding Society* and *American Sociology*. He still worked with his wonted energy, and when he died in 1954 he left three major works in process: "Mid-Century South: The New Southern Regions of the United States"; a volume on folk sociology; and an autobiographical work, "White Sands of Bethlehem."

In so brief a survey of an active and complex career, it is possible only to point to some of the ways in which the significance of Howard Odum may be felt by historians of the South. To sum it up, there are four chief areas in which he made major contributions. One was in his organizational and administrative contributions at the University of North Carolina—where he was the founder of the Department of Sociology, the School of Social Work (formerly the School of Public Welfare), the Institute for Research in Social Science, and the journal *Social Forces*. Because of these contributions alone, but also because of the students he sent out all over the South and his magic touch with the national foundations, Odum deserves to be labeled the father of the systematic scientific study of southern society. There were earlier contributions to social science, to be sure, but none had the long-range persistent effect of Odum's work.

A second contribution is in the body of his descriptive writings on the South—presenting a picture of southern folk, black and white, that is unmatched for its perceptiveness, in a range all the way from prose-poetry depiction to general statistical analysis and set in a context of historical development.

A third contribution is in a rich body of papers that can be used not only to study Odum's manifold activities, but also as sources for many aspects of southern development. No student of Negro history and race relations, for example, could afford to overlook the resources here, particularly valuable for the Commission on Interracial Cooperation and the formation of the Southern Regional Council. Nor could a student of the role of the foundations in southern life fail to use Odum's papers. Odum had notoriously successful contacts with all of the foundations, and in his correspondence can be found letters from Beardsley Ruml, Jackson Davis, Edwin R. Embree, and other foundation officers. The student of economic and political development will find illuminating information and comments, both from Odum and leaders in those fields—especially useful, perhaps, on the operation of New Deal agencies in the state of North Carolina. Buried in the manuscripts are such gems of prophetic insight as this comment, written to H. L. Mencken in 1923:

> This thing of ecclesiastical dogmatism and demagogy is one of the things that we are trying so hard to get at. I do not believe that this leadership is passing yet in a great many parts of the South. Personally, I should rather transfer the leadership gradually when we have something to substitute for it besides Atlanta commercialism. One of the most pathetic mongrel breeds of the age would be a cross between Bishop [Warren A.] Candler and W. D. Upshaw's ecclesiastical demagogy, "with the Atlanta spirit," nurtured in an environment of mass-minded folk still limited in experience, education, and opportunity, and led by Tom Watson. You can see the danger; because in each of these there would be a certain basis of sincerity and native energy.

Some indication of the scope of the papers may be gained by listing several of the more important correspondents: Will W. Alexander, H. L. Mencken, Gerald W. Johnson, Julia Collier Harris, Charles S. Johnson, C. C. Spaulding, John Temple Graves, Virginius Dabney, Barry Bingham, Mark Ethridge, Prentiss M. Terry, Donald Comer, Francis P. Miller, Benjamin B. Kendrick, George Fort Milton, Donald Davidson, Wilson Gee, H. C. Nixon, Frank P. Graham, Harry W. Chase,

Jonathan Daniels, N. C. Newbold, T. J. Woofter, Jr., George Mitchell, Cameron Morrison, J. C. B. Ehringhaus, O. Max Gardner, Clyde R. Hoey, Melville Broughton, Ralph McGill.

The fourth and greatest contribution, of course, was the Odumesque development of regionalism, not original in theory, perhaps, but original in its synthesis of the multiple currents of regionalism and significant in its popularization of the idea. In the words of Vance and Jocher: "Odum's work went further than interpreting the South to the Nation and the Nation to the South. It pointed to one possible integration of social science; it projected trends of development for the South; and it cried aloud for implementation in social action and social planning."

But what has been the influence of regionalism? What its effectiveness in the realms of action? The influence of Odum's regionalism in southern thought would be difficult to trace. Suffice it to say here that at least thousands, possibly millions, of southerners were exposed to it either directly or through pamphlets, monographs, or teachers having their origins in that school of thought. His magnum opus, *Southern Regions*, went through four printings and enjoyed such wide popularity as a textbook that a large portion of a generation of college students became familiar with the general outlines of the idea. In the social sciences the concept has had a considerable impact, as the monumental bibliography of regionalism will show. Today, however, interest has lagged, and the concept has fallen perhaps more into neglect than into dispute. The explanation for this state of affairs probably lies in the view that regionalism was primarily a program for the development of the underdeveloped southern regions. With inter-regional balance apparently approaching reality, the whole concept has somehow fallen into disuse. Region-alism has come to appear in perspective as a sort of way station on the road from southern sectionalism toward integration into the national culture—and not as a permanent phenomenon.

In the practical realm, it has scarcely any effect at all, except in so far as piecemeal programs of local and state planning may stem from Odum's emphasis upon plan-ning. Odum was frustrated in the hope during his life-time to establish a Council on Southern Regional De-velopment that would push the "national-regional" approach to take the place of the "sectional-local." Nor was any serious application ever made of his idea of official regional-planning agencies to complement na-tional and state planning boards. There is no program for overall regional planning. Such limited agencies as do exist, most notably the Southern Regional Edu-cation Board, the various industrial groups, the aca-demic and professional associations, and the Southern Regional Council are so specialized in their purposes, and sometimes so sectional in their outlook, as to fall far short of what Howard Odum envisioned.

A part of the responsibility for this condition must be assigned to Odum himself. He suffered from the occu-pational hazard of academicians (not only sociologists), difficulty in expressing his advanced concepts with absolute clarity, in his case partly because of his addic-tion to sociological terminology; but also partly because he never reached the ultimate synthesis and explanation of his ideas. There may also be some suspicion that he suffered from an academic timidity that made it difficult for him to express his ideas with full clarity because he inwardly shrank from the controversies they would inspire—and from their inevitable corollary of political action. That he could achieve clarity is evident from the heights of artistry he reached at times. But he was the victim of an active mind that raced on from one thing to another, and would not always stop to go back and polish up his drafts. Consequently, he wrote more perhaps than he should have, and published practically all of it. His organizational and administrative work also suffered from the excessive diffusion of energy.

The difficulty in reading some of his writings, however, cannot be any excuse for neglecting them. His deep love for the South and its people, combined with an acute, analytical mind, made him the most perceptive observer of the southern scene during the first half of the twentieth century. He saw it whole, the old and new, the folk and the academic, the agrarian and the industrial, the spiteful and the generous—and saw it all with a profound sensitivity and respect.

Howard Odum was a scholar in the grand manner. In him the folk heritage of the New South coalesced with intellectual insights into new concepts of universal import. He was a rare academic specimen whose scholarship had practical implications that he himself sought to apply in social action. Beyond the surveys and theory, he looked and planned toward a better future in which the South should not set its face against the world with periodic forays into sectionalism, but would seek to blend modern techniques of social science with the best of its folkways to create "a South capable and willing to work out its economic, social, and political problems by means of scientific methods and persistent efforts . . . an American South of continuing and new achievements . . . representative of the best that America could produce."

6

The Southern Strategy:
A Historical Perspective

THE MORE IT CHANGES—THE MORE IT IS THE SAME THING.
That familiar French proverb is said to have originated
with an obscure novelist and political satirist named
Alphonse Karr. During the French Revolution of 1848,
which eventually swept Napoleon III to power, Karr became oppressed with a sense of watching history repeat
itself: "After so many commotions and changes, it is
time to recognize one thing, that it is as in a cabaret:
green label, red label, etc.—One changes sometimes the
price, sometimes the cork, but it is always the same sour
wine that one has us drink.—The more it changes—
the more it is the same thing."

In the decade of the 1960s southerners like the
Frenchman could have moments when it seemed as if
they had come full circle to the replay of a historical
drama first enacted a century before. The Civil War
Centennial remained a period-piece played out in cos-
tume, without live ammunition. The Reconstruction
centennial, however, was staged in modern dress, if a
little ahead of schedule. The pageantry was absent: we

failed to reenact the impeachment of President Johnson and forgot to observe 1970 as the centennial of the Fifteenth Amendment, which guaranteed Negro suffrage. One could easily strain the point by seeking out specific parallels, but the issues of Reconstruction, to a greater degree than the issues of the Civil War, have remained live issues in the twentieth century.

Some years ago historian Crane Brinton, in his *Anatomy of Revolution*, sought to chart certain stages and forces common to all revolutions, up to the reaction with which they end. If one could assume a parallel in the anatomy of Reconstruction, one might reason that in the late 1960s the civil rights revolution reached the stage of Thermidorean reaction, or in the anatomy of Reconstruction the Hayes administration with which it ended. The parallel is a tempting one: Rutherford B. Hayes had a "southern policy"; Richard M. Nixon had a "southern strategy." The southern strategy, like the southern policy, dictated a posture of neglect toward the aspirations of black Americans. It foretokens, therefore, a cycle of reaction and repression. It foretokens, moreover, a new Solid South, this time Republican instead of Democratic, or so one might have thought before the midterm elections of 1970.

Such parallels are tempting, and they can serve a useful purpose unless they run out of control. Historical analogy can point up possibilities and highlight dangers; it cannot supply a science of prophecy. Our times are so different from the times of Rutherford Hayes that it would be difficult to believe that history will follow the same sequel, either in civil rights or in patterns of voting. Perhaps one should not strain the analogy much beyond the point that Nixon, like Hayes, sought to cultivate conservative sentiment by relaxing or appearing to relax the commitment to legal rights newly achieved in principle by the black minority—and, in the light of the 1970 elections, with little more apparent success than Hayes.

Cautionary words about historical analogy, however, may be misplaced in the age of pop-art culture. Danger lurks in the misuse of historical example, but danger lurks also in the demand for the relevant, which is often to say the shallow and the ephemeral. This is the danger that lurks in the social sciences—the "ologies": sociology, psychology, anthropology, and now the newest entry in the field, "psephology." Recently this barbaric neologism has crept almost undetected into the American language: *psephology*, from a Greek word meaning *ballots*, hence the study of ballots or of voting behavior. The chief function of this new coinage, apparently, is to give a scientific cachet to one of the major branches of fortune-telling—reading the entrails of voters and foretelling the outcome of elections, an industry that promises to outstrip Kremlinology in its gross product.

Recently three major creations have rolled off the psephological assembly lines, along with countless compact models: the sensation of 1969 was *The Emerging Republican Majority*, by Kevin P. Phillips; the new models for 1970 were *The Hidden Crisis in American Politics*, by Samuel Lubell, and *The Real Majority*, by Richard C. Scammon and Ben J. Wattenberg. *The Emerging Republican Majority*, widely celebrated as the manifesto of the southern strategy, proved to be a nine-days' wonder that perfectly illustrated the hazards of prophecy. Kevin P. Phillips—a young lawyer, a former Nixon campaign worker, a former special assistant to the attorney general, more recently a columnist—predicted that the true majority in the United States for the remainder of the twentieth century would be conservative and Republican, with its bastions in the South and in the "heartland" of the Plains and Rocky Mountains. A new era had begun, Phillips told us: "The long-range meaning of the political upheaval of 1968 rests on the Republican opportunity to fashion a majority among the 57 per cent of the American electorate which voted to eject the Democratic Party from national power," that is, the 57 percent who voted for Richard Nixon or George Wallace. A fitting epigraph for the book, one reviewer thought, would be George Wallace's rallying cry: "They's more of us than they is of them."

Phillips' argument depended first upon an ethnic interpretation of American politics and a projection of voting trends among ethnic groups, mostly toward the Republican party; second, upon a view that major realignments in American politics have occurred at regular intervals; and third, upon a more dubious argument that the tides of change in American politics have arisen from a South and West in rebellion against successive northeastern "establishments" (the latest of which is the New Deal-Liberal establishment). The first two of these interpretations followed themes currently fashionable among political scientists and historians. One was an emphasis upon ethnic factors in voting—Phillips argued that white ethnic groups had been "trending" away from the Democrats in revulsion against black militants and the "liberal establishment," particularly that establishment's rebellious children. The other theme was the study of "party systems" in American history.

On this Phillips followed what have become fairly

standard groupings. For some reason he omitted the Federalist-Jeffersonian Republican system which originated in the 1790s (say 1796, with the first partisan presidential election); but after that he noted the Democratic-Whig system which arose soon after Andrew Jackson's victory in 1828; the Democratic-Republican system which emerged with Lincoln in 1860; and then without change of party names, the cycle of Republican supremacy after 1896 (the election of McKinley) and Democratic supremacy after 1932 (the election of Franklin D. Roosevelt). This reckoning carried a symmetry that is strangely perfect: five cycles of politics, each lasting thirty-two or thirty-six years, during each of which members of the "out" party occupied the White House only eight years—in the tenures of the two Adamses, Harrison, Tyler, Taylor, Fillmore, Cleveland, Wilson, and Eisenhower. Perhaps this denotes some organic cycle of rise and fall—or perhaps another "ology," "numerology"—but Phillips reasoned that every thirty-two or thirty-six years a major realignment occurs in the American political universe. Take 1932, add thirty-six years and one reaches 1968. Richard Nixon, ipso facto, heralded a new era of Republican supremacy!

For all the minutiae of ethnic and political history, for all the historical maps and tables and statistics with which Phillips garnished his text, his projections emerged from a flattened perspective in which the future became an extension of the year 1968. If that prospect seems less than appealing one should remember that four years earlier the soothsayers were drawing their projections from the defeat of Barry Goldwater and foretelling the everlasting Democratic majority.

The prudent political prophet, perhaps, must take a cue from J. P. Morgan who, when asked once what the market would do, responded: "It will fluctuate." And indeed both of the more recent books, by Lubell and by Scammon and Wattenberg, anticipate more fluctuation at the polls than Phillips. Neither accepts his supposition that in the long run the Wallace voter belongs necessarily to the Republicans, and both books question whether the peculiar "social issue" of 1968 and 1970 can be monopolized by one party.

The historian, of course, can view all this with a certain wry detachment, for the historian seldom runs the risk of prophecy. He knows, perhaps too well, the snares set for the unwary, the hopes unfulfilled, the trends overlooked, the ironic turns of fortune when events get in the saddle. He suspects, too, that the turn in Republican fortunes below the Potomac during the last two decades owes less to new strategies than to new conditions, for the southern strategy was not born yesterday. It was invented—or at least first pursued—in the 1870s by Rutherford B. Hayes, who called it his southern policy. And subsequent changes have been only variations on a theme by Hayes.

To understand the southern policy of Hayes, one must turn briefly to even earlier times. The most casual student of southern history should know that the antebellum South briefly developed a vigorous two-party competition. Its duration, however, spanned little more than the decade of the 1840s and the "party system" never became institutionalized in the antebellum South. After the Federalists, only the short-lived Whig party made a serious challenge to the dominant party, and that for less than two decades.

The Whig party, born of opposition to Andrew Jackson in the 1830s, embraced diverse elements which favored both nationalism and states' rights, those who disliked Jackson's rebuffs to the national bank and national roads and those who disliked his stand against nullification. Both North and South, the Whigs had a reputation for respectability, for association with the "broadcloth" element. In the South they embraced the black-belt planters (the "cotton snobs"), the urban merchants and bankers, but also, especially in North Carolina, the mountaineers who needed roads and supported the party of internal improvements. The southern Whigs soon became, like their northern partners, mainly the party of Henry Clay, the Kentucky nationalist who championed an "American System" of tariffs, national bank, and internal improvements, and the Great Compromiser who championed sectional peace.

Thus southern whiggery, while not synonymous with Unionism, became permeated with Unionism. When sectional controversy over slavery disrupted the Whig party in the 1850s as it would disrupt the Democratic party in 1860, southern Whigs persisted in efforts to save the union, supported John Bell of Tennessee on the Constitutional Union ticket in 1860, stood among the foes of secession, and after secession joined the champions of compromise.

The studies of "persistent Whiggery" by Professor Thomas B. Alexander give testimony to the survival of whiggish sentiments in the Confederacy and on into the postwar South. Whig Unionism gained influence as disillusionment with secession mounted, and old Whigs after the war dominated most of the state governments under presidential Reconstruction. At that point, Alexander argues, the southern Whigs missed the chance to shape a national coalition of moderate Unionists. Instead they achieved division when the new state governments under Andrew Johnson passed the restrictive black codes and elected Confederate brigadiers to Congress. Many of the brigadiers were old Unionists who had opposed secession, but that point was lost in the polarization between Johnson and the Radical Republicans.

Even so, once the Radical triumph was assured, more than a few Whigs found enough whiggery in the Republican program to justify support and reasoned that by joining the party they could moderate its more extreme elements. The outstanding example was James L. Alcorn, a conservative planter who became the first Republican governor of Mississippi before he lost out to a Negro-carpetbagger faction. Most of the old Whigs, however, found themselves drawn to the Democratic party, which commonly reorganized under the name Conservative to accommodate the new recruits. "The circumstances now surrounding the *South*," wrote the editor of Mississippi's *Hinds County Gazette* in 1868, ". . . are of such vast importance, and the lines so fairly drawn between the Radicals and Democrats, that the Whigs of the South cannot do otherwise than vote with the Democrats, though they do so under protest." Northern Republicans, as well as southern Democrats, assumed a whiggish cast with the waning of Reconstruction. In 1876–1877 the circumstances of the disputed presidential election made possible an effort to bring this harmony of outlook into play, to split off southern

Democrats from northern, and to arrange the compromise which permitted Hayes to become president.

The elements of compromise need only brief review
here. The dispute turned on contested electoral votes
from three southern states: Florida, Louisiana, South
Carolina. The Constitution had not anticipated the
question, and Congress was divided between a Republican Senate and Democratic House. A special electoral
commission, unique in American history, recommended
a decision for Hayes, but House Democrats threatened
a filibuster, whereupon friends of Hayes and a group of
southerners met in the Wormley House, a Washington
hotel, to strike a bargain; the southerners would let
Hayes take office and would accept in good faith the
Reconstruction amendments; Hayes, in turn, would
remove federal troops protecting Republican state governments in South Carolina and Louisiana. Behind this
agreement, however, lay more complicated economic
and political understandings about federal aid for the
Texas and Pacific Railroad, money for internal improvements in the South, a cabinet appointment for a
southerner, and a more tenuous agreement for Republican James A. Garfield to become Speaker of the House
despite a thin Democratic majority.

In retrospect, the sequel to the compromise seems inevitable. Yet the new president had shown enough prag-
matism to suggest that in different circumstances he
would have pursued different options. A moderate antislavery Whig who joined the Republicans and fought
for the Union, Hayes had voted with the Radicals in
Congress, but later expressed disillusionment with Reconstruction policies. As governor of Ohio he became
known as a reformer but remained loyal to Ulysses S.

Grant. Before his nomination for president Hayes spoke of the need for sectional reconciliation, but during the campaign he encouraged party leaders to wave the "bloody shirt." "Our strong ground is the dread of a solid South, rebel rule, etc. etc.," he wrote to James G. Blaine. "I hope you will make these topics prominent in your speeches. It leads people away from 'hard times' which is our deadliest foe." The campaign betrayed little hint of the southern policy he would pursue as president.

When the first returns signaled a defeat, Hayes confessed: "I do not care for myself . . . but I do care for the poor colored men of the South. . . . The Southern people will practically treat the constitutional amendments as nullities, and then the colored man's fate will be worse than when he was in slavery." By this Hayes meant to predict the result of a Democratic victory; ironically he had predicted the result of his own. The circumstances of the electoral dispute soon put Hayes in a posture of conciliation toward southern Democrats and thereby pushed him toward a policy that perhaps better fitted his temperament than his convictions.

Once inaugurated he set about appeasing southern whites, largely, it turned out, by deserting southern blacks. Federal troops withdrew from the state houses in South Carolina and Louisiana. David M. Key, a Tennessean of conservative bent, became postmaster general and directed a patronage policy that decimated Republican organizations in the South. A practice which confirmed if it did not induce the collapse of the Republican party became quickly rationalized as an effort to rebuild the party on a new basis. By stressing a whiggish policy of internal improvements and sectional peace,

Hayes reasoned, by naming "respectable" whites to federal offices, he could lure enough intelligent and propertied whites (especially old Whigs and Unionists) to transform the Republican party, but without losing the support of the freedmen. More hope than policy, perhaps, the plan resembled the program of Benjamin Disraeli, who sponsored an alliance of the British gentry and masses in a national party which played both ends against the middle. When Hayes advised blacks in Atlanta that their "rights and interests would be safer if . . . intelligent white men were let alone by the general government," he expressed not so much a platitude as a real trust that white men of intelligence and property would behave with equity toward the less fortunate. More than that, he reasoned that division in the white vote and competition for the black vote would best protect human rights in the long run. "The whites must be divided there," Hayes wrote in his diary, "before a better state of things will prevail."

It was not an ignoble design, but neither was it an idea whose time had come. It was an idea whose time had passed with the advent of Radical Reconstruction. Whatever opportunity may have existed in 1865 had dissolved in the next twelve years. The southern policy of Hayes proposed a shift in attitudes, allegiances, and party labels too sudden to be achieved. The Republican organizations in the South—decimated by defeat, starved for patronage, and hostile to his purpose—gave Hayes little or no machinery with which to pursue his goal. Thus, his southern policy was all strategy and no tactics.

Its effect was to dishearten Republicans and embolden Democrats who busily reinforced their control. Federal appointments seduced few Democrats. In fact, appointees often affirmed their Democratic allegiance the more fiercely, in self-defense. As if to compound the irony, black-belt Democrats soon effected the very alliance of top and bottom that Hayes had sought. In some areas their economic and social power enabled white Democrats to preside over a controlled black electorate. The party of white supremacy, paradoxically, would soon use black votes to overcome white majorities that favored Independents and Populists.

Hayes's design to dish the Democrats barely survived the summer of 1877. In September he made a swing through the middle South, accompanied much of the way by South Carolina's Wade Hampton, meeting large and sympathetic audiences. But the euphoria soon faded. The honeymoon was over in October, when Congress met in special session and southern Democrats failed to permit Garfield's election as Speaker. After that Hayes expressed second thoughts about a Texas and Pacific Railroad subsidy. From that point the spirit of conciliation dissipated.

In 1878 the southern hill country caught an infection of farm radicalism from the West. The fever of greenback doctrine passed, only to rise again in later years, but it affected southern Democrats enough to immunize them against the whiggish appeals of Hayes, defender of sound currency and the public credit. During the spring of 1878 House Democrats began to investigate the previous election. They meant to embarrass Hayes, but the attempt boomeranged when the Republicans produced certain cipher dispatches that incriminated Democrats in efforts to pressure election officials.

Meanwhile Hayes met growing hostility from stalwart

Republicans like Roscoe Conkling and William E. Chandler. The president, said the abolitionist William Lloyd Garrison, "sits in his magisterial chair, serene, smiling, complacent, and confident that the best way to protect sheep from being devoured is to give them over to the custody of the wolves." As if to confirm the observation, southern Democrats rejected conciliation and revived their bulldozing tactics in the midterm elections, and a nearly solid South emerged. In the former Confederacy, state governments remained Democratic and the number of Republican congressmen fell from ten to three. Republicans bore losses in both white and black counties. In the Deep South they reached virtual collapse.

Hayes confided to his diary regret "that the better elements of the South were not . . . organized." A week after the elections he confessed to a reporter: *"I am reluctantly forced to admit that the experiment was a failure. The first election of importance held since it was attempted has proved that fair elections with free suffrage for every voter in the South are an impossibility under the existing condition of things."* Whatever his intention, the southern policy of Hayes had served little purpose except to cover his retreat. It ratified the collapse of southern Republicanism and did little to mollify the Democrats who turned their backs on conciliation. After the midterm elections they forced Hayes onto the defensive just to protect the remaining shreds of federal protection for the right to vote. Their special target was the Federal Elections Act of 1871, which authorized federal deputy marshals and supervisors to observe elections and report alleged frauds to the courts. In 1877 a Republican Senate had blocked the first attempt to repeal this safeguard, but from 1879 to 1881 the

Democratic Congress passed eight repeal bills, each of which Hayes vetoed. Reluctant to forego at least the principle of protection, Hayes continued adamant on this point, but federal supervision of elections remained only a feeble gesture until finally repealed under President Cleveland in 1894.

Both North and South drifted back into the mood of sectionalism, and stalwarts rallied to their old banner. "The bloody shirt," William Lloyd Garrison insisted. *"In hoc signo vinces."* And in that sign James A. Garfield conquered. *The Republican Campaign Text Book for 1880* gave more than half its space to bloody-shirt themes, and party propaganda played on the familiar fear of unreconstructed rebels. But the tone was defensive. There was no commitment to a renewed Reconstruction. The answer to a Solid South would be simply a Solid North. The vote in 1880 produced a Solid South in the electoral college for the first time after the Civil War—and very nearly a Solid North beyond the border states, except for California, Nevada, and New Jersey.

The first major variation on the strategy of Hayes occurred under his immediate successors. Where circumstances impelled Hayes to bid for conservative support, circumstances impelled Garfield and Arthur to fraternize with economic radicals. The political independents who sprang up in the South after Reconstruction had little in common with orthodox Republicans, except opposition to the Democrats. They endorsed a variety of heterodox proposals: debt repudiation, inflation, usury laws, antimonopoly laws. Locally they fought Bourbon Democrats over fencing laws, the dominance of courthouse rings, and a variety of personal complaints. In Virginia, where the Readjuster Movement championed readjustment of the state debt, Independents captured the legislature in 1879 and elected a governor in 1881. When the Readjusters sent their leader, William E. Mahone, to the Senate he found himself suddenly the key figure in a chamber evenly divided between the parties. To win his vote Senate Republicans came to terms, and Garfield came across with a share of the federal patronage.

When Chester Arthur became president in the fall of 1881 he broadened this qualified alliance into a policy of wholesale collaboration. "I have made up my mind that a permanently defeated Republican party is of little value," Arthur said, ". . . and that if any respectable body of men wages war on the Bourbon Democracy, with reasonable prospects of success, it should be sustained." In nearly every southern state Arthur fed patronage to Independents and urged southern Republicans to collaborate in their campaigns. In 1882 the alliance showed promise. Eight Republicans went to Congress and eight Independents, twice the number two years before, but six of the Independents were from Virginia, where the Readjusters lost control the following year. In 1884 all the Independent congressmen lost, together with Republican presidential candidate James G. Blaine, who polled a smaller proportion of the southern vote than either Hayes or Garfield.

Out of power under Cleveland, Republicans vacillated between waving the bloody shirt and cultivating sentiment for the protective tariff among New South businessmen. In 1888 Benjamin Harrison eschewed the bloody shirt and emphasized protectionism, but polled a still smaller part of the southern vote than Blaine. In

1890, having concluded that Republicans lost in the South mainly because they could not register their full strength at the polls, Harrison threw his support behind one final drive to protect the voting rights of southern Negroes. The Lodge elections bill, sponsored by Congressman Henry Cabot Lodge of Massachusetts, proposed to give federal supervisors power to control registration and pass on the qualifications of challenged voters. The "force bill," as Democrats tagged it, passed the House on a party-line vote, but was sidetracked in the Senate to make way for silver and tariff bills and was finally defeated. The will to regulate southern elections was lacking.

In 1892 when discontents of farmers South and West gave rise to the People's party, Harrison had one more chance to cultivate an Independent rebellion. In his campaign for reelection the Republican national committee sought to coordinate Republican and Populist groups, but the fusion failed to show much strength in a key test, the Georgia state elections in October, in which Populists lost out to wholesale manipulation by Democrats. Harrison was reported to have greeted the news in a furious rage. "I have washed my hands of the south," he told a visitor, if we may believe the Atlanta *Constitution*. "It is a land of rebels and traitors who care nothing for the sanctity of the ballot, and I will never be in favor of making an active campaign down there until we can place bayonets at the polls. I am now more than ever in favor of ramming a force bill down their throats." Harrison himself lost the election in November.

In four years Benjamin Harrison recapitulated the

whole history of southern strategies. He tried everything again, and again nothing worked. First, a variation
on Hayes's appeal to the conservatives, with focus on
the protective tariff. Second, a return to Radicalism with
the Lodge bill, which failed to pass. And finally, a return
to the Garfield-Arthur strategy of collaboration with
Independents, in this case with the Populists. Republican vacillation and failure were the products of many
circumstances: disillusionment with Reconstruction,
factional division, a growing doctrine of racial distinc-
tions, the influence of northern businessmen with southern connections, the various social and cultural movements toward sectional reconciliation, which meant
reconciliation of white men to the disadvantage of black.

But the persistent neglect of black Republicans won
few points with southern whites. Republicans could not
reverse the image they had acquired in the sectional
conflict. They were the northern party which had opposed the right of the South to carry slaves into the territories. They had waged war on the South, freed the
slaves, and imposed Radical Reconstruction. During the
debate over the Lodge bill in 1890 a group of southern
congressmen hastily assembled a little volume entitled
Why the Solid South? The answer they gave in 452 pages
can be summarized in one word: Reconstruction. State
by state they described that period in terms that would
shape the image of Reconstruction history for more
than fifty years. Indeed one measure of the Republican
burden was the degree to which the terminology of
Democratic propaganda dominated political discourse
and entered historiography: carpetbagger, scalawag,
home rule, the bloody shirt, "outrage mills" (a jocose

term for reports of political violence and murder), force bill, bayonets, Negro domination.

During the 1890s southern Republicans toyed with Populist alliances. In 1892 Republicans in Alabama and Louisiana arranged fusions with Populists and in other states gave their informal support or endorsement. Here and there well-known Republican names appeared on Populist tickets, and local fusions occurred. In Alabama, which proved to be the banner Populist state of the South in 1892 (36.6 percent of its presidential vote for the Populists), the "Jeffersonian Democrat" Reuben F. Kolb had Populist and Republican support for governor. In the end he lost out on the vote from black-belt counties, which the Democrats controlled. The same thing would happen again in 1894. Throughout the South in the 1892 and subsequent elections the Populists fell victim to invective, intimidation, ballot-box stuffing, vote buying, physical violence. "We had to do it!" one Georgia Democrat said years later. "Those d—— Populists would have ruined the country!"

Populism reached and passed its climax in 1896, when the Democrats under William Jennings Bryan ran off with their issue of free silver. Their decision to support Bryan then placed southern Populists in the impossible situation of favoring a Democratic candidate for president while collaborating with Republicans at the state level. In Georgia, Alabama, and Texas, Populist state tickets with Republican help polled over 40 percent of the votes even as reported by Democratic boards. In Louisiana a Republican gubernatorial candidate on a fusionist ticket probably was counted out. But in North Carolina, where fusion had carried the legislature in

1894, a new election law made it possible for fusionists to register their full strength. A straight-out Republican governor was elected, a fusionist state ticket, a fusionist legislature, and four Populist and three Republican congressmen (the House later seated a fifth Populist in a contested election). But North Carolina Democrats mobilized on the issue of white supremacy in 1898, swept the fusionists out of the legislature, and went on to elect a governor in 1900.

Populism therefore never came to power in a single southern state, and the threat posed by fusionists in the 1890s impelled the Democrats to tighten their control, to disfranchise Negro Republicans chiefly by literacy tests and other measures and the establishment of white primaries. After the turn of the century the Republican presidential vote in the South, which had held at 30 to 40 percent of the popular vote after Reconstruction, fell off sharply. The Solid South, having subdued Republicans, Independents, and Populists, would not face another sustained threat until the mid-twentieth century.

William McKinley's campaign for president illustrated perfectly the standard uses of what had become the rotten boroughs of Republicanism in the South. His campaign may almost be said to have originated in the South, at Thomasville, Georgia, whence McKinley in 1895 repaired to the vacation home of his strategist Mark Hanna, to consult quietly with southern Republicans and line up convention delegates before other candidates realized what was afoot. This strategy scored a brilliant success, but McKinley's election in 1896, which began a cycle of Republican supremacy in the nation, left the Solid South without any sustained challenge until the mid-twentieth century. Indebted to southern delegates for convention votes, McKinley outdid his predecessors in the appointment of token Negroes to office, but made little effort to develop a southern strategy for elections. During southern tours in 1898 and 1901, his appeals to white southerners were either sentimental pleas for reunion or prophecies of a rich future. "Sectional lines no longer mar the map of the United States," he told the Georgia legislature a few months after the Spanish-American War. "The old flag again waves over us in peace, with new glories which your sons and ours have added this year to its sacred folds." In the same speech he declared the care of Confederate graves a national duty.

McKinley's successor, Theodore Roosevelt, had the distinction of a southern ancestry—his mother was one of the Georgia Bullochs. But the advantage greatly diminished after Booker T. Washington came to dinner at the White House in 1901. Shortly after that incident Roosevelt wrote to Henry Cabot Lodge: "In the Southern Atlantic and Gulf States there has really been no Republican Party . . . simply a set of black and white scalawags . . . who are concerned purely in getting the Federal offices and sending to the national conventions delegates whose venality makes them a menace to the whole party." But Roosevelt, like McKinley, found that expediency required him to cultivate the existing organizations to win nomination. His most conspicuous acts in that connection, aside from public acknowledgment of Washington as patronage adviser, were to appoint a Negro, William D. Crum, collector of customs in Charleston and to close the post office in Indianola, Mississippi, after mob threats forced the black post-mistress to resign.

In 1905, after he had won election to a full term, Roosevelt tried to repair the damage among southern whites by a tour of the South, during which he eulogized General Lee and visited the ancestral Bulloch home at Roswell, but the wide popularity that he achieved won no significant political gains. "The way of Roosevelt with the South was as tortuous as the proverbial way of a man with a maid," wrote C. Vann Woodward. "Simul-taneously, or by turns, he wooed the mutually hostile Black-and-Tans, Lily-whites, and White-Supremacy Democrats." But whites could not forget Booker T. Washington's dinner at the White House, and Negroes lost faith when Roosevelt summarily discharged three companies of black troops in 1906 after a riot in Browns-ville, Texas. For all his bluster Roosevelt, like his pred-ecessors, vacillated and drifted still further toward a lily-white policy. Later, when he organized the Progres-sive party in 1912, the Bull Moose convention refused to seat any Negro delegates from the South.

Under William Howard Taft a brief but illusory gain in southern Republicanism occurred. The growth of the industrial New South continued to enlarge the business groups sympathetic to Republican economic policies on currency and the tariff, and hostile to the populistic Democracy of William Jennings Bryan. Southern pub-licists like William Garrott Brown and Walter Hines Page began to call for a dissolution of the Solid South. In October, 1908, Taft became the first presidential candidate of his party to carry his campaign into the South—on a tour through Kentucky, Tennessee, North

Carolina, and Virginia. The Republican vote increased significantly in those and other southern states, and even brought Taft close to victory in Tennessee and North Carolina. North Carolina sent three Republicans to Congress. Taft ventured a prediction after the election that three or four southern states would go Republican in the next election and in a speech assured the North Carolina Society of New York that Republicans would not interfere with Negro disfranchisement. In 1909 an extensive tour carried Taft into every southern state except Florida, but mainly for ceremonial occasions at which he, like McKinley, gave audiences what they wanted to hear—praise of southern traditions and southern heroes. Taft nominated southern Democrats to federal offices, appointed fewer Negroes than any of his predecessors, called upon southern businessmen to support Republican economic policies, and openly endorsed white supremacy; but his position on the tariff proved highly unpopular in the region, and Democrats swept the midterm elections. Taft's personal popularity in the South, like Roosevelt's, produced no political gains. In 1912 the nation turned to Woodrow Wilson, the first Democrat president elected since 1892, with comfortable majorities throughout the South.

In 1920 the landslide victory of Warren Harding brought another rise in the southern Republican vote, enough to carry the state of Tennessee, probably because the party won credit for the state's ratification of woman suffrage. "Mr. Harding thinks the time is ripe for dissolving the Solid South," the still hopeful William Howard Taft reported after the election. But Harding remained impaled on the horns of the old Republican dilemma: how to combine a growing white vote with a traditional black vote. With some apparent hope that he could find the formula to get a few more Negro votes in the South without antagonizing whites, Harding seized upon the occasion of the semicentennial of Birmingham, Alabama, in 1921 to deliver a speech on the race question. The strategy was to "stand uncompromisingly against every suggestion of social equality" but to argue that the black man should vote "when he is fit to vote" and have equal opportunities "in precisely the same way and to the same extent . . . as between members of the same race." Even so mild, almost platitudinous, a speech met widespread hostility among both whites and blacks, and effected little or no change in the political situation. After Harding's death, Calvin Coolidge said even less on the subject. Both men endorsed federal antilynching bills, but neither restored Negro patronage to pre-Wilson levels or acted against the segregation established in government offices under Wilson. And neither acted with any vigor to devise a successful southern strategy. That remained for Coolidge's successor, Herbert Hoover, who tried to foster a lily-white Republicanism "of such character as would commend itself to the citizens of those states." But Hoover, the herald of prosperity, became the victim of adversity and the party of reconstruction became the party of depression.

The story of Republican efforts to build a party in the South, then, was a story of futility, a futility born chiefly of the failure of Reconstruction. Republicans over the years progressively abandoned the Radical tradition which, however, still hung like an albatross around their necks. Republican presidents appointed southern Democrats to federal office, neglected southern Negroes, and called on the New South to support their economic policies. But the more it changed—the more it was the same thing. The more Republicans abandoned the black man—the more they failed with the white. Yet all Republican presidents remained dependent for convention votes upon regular organizations that included Negroes, and ambivalence about Negro Republicans continued.

Not until the mid-twentieth century would the southern policy of Rutherford B. Hayes begin to score success. It would come with Eisenhower, but less because of any new southern strategy than because of new conditions that afflicted the Democrats with severe internal tensions. In the 1930s the Democrats undermined the Republican loyalties of black voters and created a new tradition of black Democrats. Among southern whites this and other departures under Democratic rule eroded the loyalties born of Civil War and Reconstruction and brought on a disruption of southern Democracy. Since the Dixiecrat rebellion of 1948 the Solid South has divided its vote in every presidential election. Eisenhower carried four states of the old Confederacy in 1952 and five in 1956. Nixon carried three in 1960 and five in 1968 (George C. Wallace another five), and in between Goldwater carried five Deep South states in 1964.

In several ways the circumstances of recent elections have paralleled the circumstances faced by Hayes and his successors. Hayes cultivated conservative and whiggish southerners; Eisenhower and Nixon scored heavily among their modern counterparts in suburban elephant jungles like Charlotte's Myers Park. Garfield, Arthur, and Harrison cultivated agrarian Independents; Gold-

water scored with modern Independents: Dixiecrats
and Wallaceites. Hayes and the others did not exactly
pursue black voters, but expected to hold the Negro
vote for the Republican party; Eisenhower managed to
score among black voters, especially in 1956, even while
he swept the silk-stocking precincts. Not until Barry
Goldwater in 1964 did a Republican candidate overtly
spurn the Negro vote.

The drift of party politics may depend mainly upon
two groups that suggest parallels to the Independents
and freedmen of the nineteenth century: some five million Wallace voters and some three million (potentially
five million) black voters, the groups that feel most aggrieved at the policies of the past. Regarding the Wallaceites—aside from the most dogmatic conservatives
among them—enough has been said by current pundits
about the tug between voting one's prejudices and voting one's pocketbook to suggest that Democratic loyalties die hard. Southern strategists have food for thought
in the recent observation of a South Carolinian: "There
ain't that many Republicans in South Carolina, just a
lot of mad Democrats." And in trying to reach mad
Democrats, Republicans will have to work against their
twentieth-century image as the party of depression (if no
longer of Reconstruction), as what a Democratic circu-
lar in Mississippi a few years ago called "a silk stocking
type that hold Coca-Cola and coffee drinking parties in
the big houses on the hill."

Republicans may find it easier to revive the traditional
support of black southerners. It is hard to believe that
black voters will be written off permanently by the party
that was their traditional home before Franklin Roose-

velt (which today has the only Negro senator) and that, even after Goldwater, carried a substantial vote among Negroes for statewide candidates in Arkansas, Tennessee, and Virginia. The need for votes in party battles will invite an appeal to black voters by both parties, and such a development could vindicate the belief of Rutherford Hayes that a political division in the white South would be the best guarantee of civil rights for the black South.

7

Business Progressivism:
Southern Politics in the Twenties

"FUNDAMENTALISM, KU KLUXRY, REVIVALS, LYNCHINGS, hog wallow politics—these are the things that always occur to a northerner when he thinks of the south." Thus spake Mencken in 1924. In this and a hundred other catalogs of southern grotesqueries on which he wielded his meat-ax in the clever twenties, Mencken contributed mightily to a neo-abolitionist image of the savage South. And he was mightily assisted by great multitudes of southerners who swarmed into the Ku Klux and fundamentalist movements, to a degree that the peculiar forces of nativism and repression seemed to have, if not their native seat, at least their major centers of influence and power in the South of the twenties. The hypnotic power of certain arresting events—the Democratic convention of 1924, the Scopes trial, the election of 1928—have given Ku Kluxry and fundamentalism the appearance of dominating southern politics to such a degree that more permanently significant developments have been overshadowed. Southern politicians, it is true, for the most part tried to avoid offending those forces—yet few were owned by them. Neither movement ever perfected the machinery to dominate any southern state to the extent that the Klan briefly dominated Indiana; neither movement was responsible for any extensive program of legislation; neither had much durability—at least as a major political force.

Any serious attempt to understand southern politics in the twenties must begin with recognition that the progressive urge of previous decades did not disappear but was transformed through an emphasis upon certain of its tendencies to the neglect of others, that in its new form progressivism pervaded southern politics of the twenties. Outrageous as the statement may seem at first, both Austin Peay, who signed the Tennessee antievolution act, and Bibb Graves, the Alabama Klan candidate in 1926, were authentic progressive governors of the twenties. In order to demonstrate this, it is not necessary to fall back upon the interpretation advanced by Richard Hofstadter and others, that the peculiar forces represented by fundamentalism and the Klan constituted a degradation of the progressive drive for moral reform. The relationship doubtless was there, but other, and more positive, continuities of progressivism may be traced into the twenties.

A growing interest in this approach among historians was pointed up in an article by Arthur S. Link in the *American Historical Review*, "What Happened to the Progressive Movement in the 1920's?" In contrast to the traditional textbook hypothesis that progressivism was submerged under a tide of revulsion against idealism and reform, Link has indicated a number of continuities and suggested other areas for exploration. This essay pursues one avenue of continuity: progressivism in southern state government.

We need first a working definition of *progressivism*. Although we speak of a progressive "movement," actually we have reference to the spirit of the age rather than to an organized movement—much as when we speak of Jacksonian democracy. A dictionary definition of anything so amorphous is impossible, but certain salient tendencies of the progressive spirit can be readily identified. One was democracy: reforms such as the party primary sought to bring government closer to the people. Second, efficiency: good government meant not only democracy but reorganization to eliminate waste. Third, corporate regulation: governmental action was urged against corporate abuses and the threat of monopoly. Fourth, social justice: a variety of reforms were encouraged, from labor legislation to prohibition. Fifth and finally, the public service concept of government: governmental responsibilities were extended into a wide range of direct services to the people—good roads, education, public health and welfare, rural credits, conservation, among others.

Two of these themes were highlighted and extended in the twenties: efficiency and public services. The other three were dimmed or partially eclipsed: democracy, corporate regulation, and social justice.

The transition from a militant democratic and anti-corporation progressivism in the early twentieth century, as described by C. Vann Woodward, to the progressivism of expansion and efficiency in the twenties was already apparent in the Wilson era. Several factors served paradoxically to make progressivism more pervasive and at the same time to temper its militancy. It fell out that Wilsonian progressivism was associated in nearly every one of its major measures with the name of one or more southerners, from the Underwood-Simmons tariff to the Smith-Hughes Act for aid to education. Powerful forces wedded even reluctant southerners to the Wilsonian leadership: the need for a party record of achievement, the spirit of party regularity, the use of the patronage, the existence of progressive factions in the southern states. The entire effect was to "Wilsonize" the southern Democratic party much as it had been "Bryanized" before, to make progressivism the fashion, but with the result of thinning down somewhat its reform urge by reliance upon a relatively conservative leadership in the Congress.

The anticorporation drive was further diluted by the cold, pure springs of prohibition. Building upon the general moral disrepute of saloons, the prohibitionists were able somehow to equate the "liquor traffic" with rural and progressive suspicion of the trusts and "special interests." When reform pressures built up, an easy outlet was through the advocacy of prohibition. For the churches, prohibition could easily become "a surrogate for the Social Gospel."

> In a peculiarly satisfying way [Dewey Grantham has written], the growing agitation over the liquor question absorbed the yearnings for reform and fulfillment of a people whose God had become Progress but whose basic ideas remained fundamentally conservative. No other proposal expressed the ambivalent desires of the South so well, nor did any other so effectively combine the varied reform elements that were struggling to assert themselves.

The militant tone of progressivism was weakened not

alone by the adherence of belated Wilsonians and prohibitionists. To quote Grantham again, "The force of
progressivism was blunted by the widespread faith in
industrial progress." The middle-class leaders who gave
progressivism its predominant tone had fought largely
against "monopoly" and railroad practices that they
thought inhibited economic development. They were
not hostile to the factory and corporation as such; and
faced with the need for outside capital, with the com-
plexity and difficulty of corporate regulation, they gradually turned their attention in the direction of prohibition, good government, and public services. In their zeal
for efficiency and expansion, in fact, the progressives
manifested the principal features of business development itself.

By the twenties, the long-heralded industrial New
South had entered what might today be called its "take-
off" period. It was the period during which southern
textiles finally took the lead from those in New England;
hydroelectric power sparked industrial revolution in the
Southeast, and petroleum did the same for the Southwest—a period during which industry and urbanization
rapidly altered the face of the land. The urban transformation inspired Gerald Johnson to write that in a
hundred towns from the Potomac to the Rio Grande
"There is no God but Advertising, and Atlanta is his
prophet." It was a period of triumph for the "Atlanta
spirit," the spirit of progress. "Conservatism," Maristan
Chapman wrote in 1922, "has become a term of reproach." But now the term *progress* appeared in a subtly
different context. It was more closely associated with
the urban middle class, with chambers of commerce and

Rotary Clubs. It carried the meaning of efficiency and development rather than of reform. In Asheville, North Carolina, Thomas Wolfe wrote his mother in 1923, they "shout 'Progress, Progress, Progress'—when what they mean is more Ford automobiles, more Rotary Clubs, more Baptist Ladies Social unions." "Greater Asheville" meant "100,000 by 1930." The "progressive" community now was the community that had good governments, great churches, improved schools, industry and business, real estate booms. The reform urge, the social justice movement, never strong in the South, had been muted; the drive to regulate corporations had all but disappeared. The old agrarian battle cries against big business and Wall Street subsided with the passing of the Farmers' Union from the southern scene and the rise of "business" methods in agriculture. Progressivism in the age of normalcy had become almost synonymous with the Atlanta spirit. Lyle H. Lanier, one of the original Vanderbilt Agrarians, wrote in 1930: "A steady barrage of propaganda issues through newspapers, magazines, radios, billboards, and other agencies . . . to the effect that progress must be maintained. It requires little sagacity to discover that progress usually turns out to mean business."

If, however, militant progressivism had been diluted by the need for capital, by chasing after the elusive goal of prohibition, and to some degree even by the Wilsonian policies, one thing is certain: by 1920 new responsibilities of the state had become a familiar part of the political landscape. Progressivism had conquered the old dictum that that government is best which governs least, whatever political rhetoric might be heard to the contrary, and had left the more extreme doctrines of limited government as dead as Yancey and Rhett. Out of two decades of progressive ferment and reform the great fundamental residue of the progressive era in southern government was the firm establishment and general acceptance of the public service function of government. It is in this respect that southern progressivism marked the great departure from the era that went before, making the twenties a decade of fruition and harvest.

The outlook of what we may now call the business progressivism of the twenties was summarized in a perceptive article by H. C. Nixon in 1931 in the *Annals of the American Academy of Political and Social Science*:

> The business class political philosophy of the new South is broad enough to include programs of highway improvement, educational expansion, and health regulation. But it does not embrace any comprehensive challenge to laissez faire ideas in the sphere of relationship between capital and labor, and the section is lagging in social support of such matters as effective child labor regulation and compensation legislation. [On the theme of efficiency, Nixon found] an influence toward change in the meaning and spirit of government as against the rather political and theoretical concepts of the country lawyer. . . . Business methods in government tend to get the right of way over the ideas of checks and balances, and governmental functions tend to expand in response to social or business needs. . . . Government tends to become an agent of industrial prosperity, with urban elements modifying the agrarian content of politics. Even professional politicians, attaining power to exploit government, do so in the name of "progress."

These trends were manifested in a number of business-

progressive governors in the twenties—a relatively col-
orless group on the whole, respectable and circum-
spect in demeanor, conservatively "constructive" in their
approach to public problems, storming no citadels of
intrenched "privilege," but carrying forward the new
public functions that had gained acceptance in the progressive era, especially good roads and schools. Good
government was for them almost a fetish. Sometimes
this attitude took the rhetorical form of political cries
for economy, but upon closer examination economy
usually meant the elimination of waste rather than the
reduction of services, and expenditures climbed rapidly.
Not always did they use economy even as a rhetorical
device. "Economy," "reduce taxes," "abolish useless
offices and reduce salaries," Governor Thomas E. Kilby
of Alabama warned as he left office in 1923; "these cries
may be popular, but . . . they contain a positive and
serious menace to the welfare of Alabama and particularly to her educational and health interests and to the
unfortunate and helpless wards of the State. Not only
do they threaten those interests but they threaten our
agricultural and industrial interests as well." That same
year the *Southern Textile Bulletin* of Charlotte ran an
editorial headed EXPENDITURES PRODUCE PROSPERITY.
"The man who is educated," it argued, "starts new
enterprises or engages in new lines of business that pay
taxes." Good roads opened new markets for farmers
and improved economic conditions. Strange doctrine, in
retrospect, for the most conservative organ of the textile
industry to be advocating, in effect, that the state should
spend its way into prosperity!

North Carolina was at the forefront of the movement,
and it was more in the twenties than in the so-called

progressive era that the state established its reputation as "the Wisconsin of the South," the leading progressive state of the region. It was during this period that it developed, under President Harry Woodburn Chase, the leading state university in the South; embarked upon the most ambitious highway program in the South; and developed extensive programs in education, public health, and welfare. In the war and postwar years the state had a succession of governors—Thomas W. Bickett, Cameron Morrison, and Angus W. McLean— who carried forward a consistent tradition of moderate progressivism reaching from Charles B. Aycock at the turn of the century. In the active expansion of public services North Carolina set the pace for other southern states and ranked high in the nation at large. Several fiscal indexes will establish the point. Between 1913 and 1930, taxes in North Carolina increased by 554 percent, a rate of increase exceeded only by Delaware. Expenditures by the state increased 847 percent between 1915 and 1925. This rate of increase was greater than in any other state, substantially more than double the national average. In total expenditure North Carolina ranked tenth among all the states in 1925, fourth in total state debt, second in per capita state debt. The total state bonded debt increased from $13,300,000 in 1920 to $178,265,000 in 1930.

The great era of expansion came after 1920, but it had its beginnings in the administration of Governor Bickett, 1917–1921. That period saw, among other things, the creation of a state public welfare system in 1917, the state guarantee of a six-month school term in 1919, and increasing expenditures for salaries, public health, and state institutions. In 1919/1920 Bickett sponsored a reorganization of the tax system that involved allocation of the general property tax to local and county uses, extension of the income tax to incomes from property, and a revaluation of property that doubled the assessments from 1919 to 1921. Increases in income taxes brought receipts from that source in 1926 almost twelve times those in 1920, constituting nearly half the state revenues. Inheritance, license, privilege, franchise, automobile, and gasoline levies all were increased during the twenties.

It was Cameron Morrison, however, who in the face of postwar depression led the great expansion. With revivalistic zeal, in his 1921 inaugural address he called upon the forces of "progressive democracy" to "war for righteousness with the reactionary and unprogressive forces of our State." In the face of his crusade for highways and schools, the reactionary forces faltered, and the legislature in 1921 approved a $50,000,000 bond issue for state highways, nearly $6,750,000 for state educational and charitable institutions, and $5,000,000 for school buildings. Before the end of Morrison's administration a total of $65,000,000 in bonds had been voted for highways, $33,718,700 appropriated for benevolent and educational institutions, public school expenditures more than doubled, and public school property tripled.

Under the direction of Frank Page, chairman of the highway commission after his return from wartime road engineering in France, administration of the highway program was kept reasonably free from political manipulation and graft. Within seven years the highway commission spent $153,546,677; developed a state system of 7,551 miles, 3,738 of which were hard-surfaced; and reclaimed "lost provinces" behind the mountains and the coastal swamps. North Carolina's act of faith was recompensed by increased revenues from gasoline and automobile taxes, enough to cover the cost. The state ended the decade second only to Texas in the South and eleventh in the nation in total mileage of surfaced roads.

The contribution of Morrison's successor, McLean, successful banker and lawyer of Lumberton, was foreshadowed in his inaugural promise to give the state "an administration characterized by efficiency, economy, and rational progress." McLean carried forward, even expanded, the programs set in motion by Morrison, but emphasized efficiency, inaugurated an executive budget system, and through other measures sought to insure fiscal regularity in the growing activities of the state.

If North Carolina was most consistent in the support of progressive governors and programs, other states moved significantly in the same direction. A transitional figure in Alabama was Thomas E. Kilby, a wealthy Anniston manufacturer. Indorsed by the Anti-Saloon League in 1918, he was swept into office on a wave of enthusiasm for the Eighteenth Amendment. His victory revitalized Alabama progressivism, and Kilby proceeded methodically and doggedly to the redemption of elaborate campaign pledges. Presented originally as a potential "business governor," he directed the establishment of a state budget system and reorganization of the tax system. State services were extended and reforms enacted in many directions, including the administrative reform of the school system after a systematic survey and the highest appropriations for public education to that time; the establishment of a state child welfare department; a reorganization of the prison system, including construction of a new penitentiary; sizable increases in appropriations for public health; a workmen's compensation law; and a $25,000,000 bond issue for roads.

After a fallow period under Governor William W. "Plain Bill" Brandon, who promised no increases in taxes but carried ahead programs started by Kilby, Alabama progressives entered another period of rapid development under Bibb Graves. Elected in 1926, he presided over another great forward surge in the last years of prosperity: another $25,000,000 road bond issue, the creation of a state bridge corporation, expansion of public schools and state colleges, added support to hospitals and charitable institutions, the achievement of national leadership in the percentage of rural population covered by full-time health service, increased support to the child welfare departments, and further development of the port of Mobile. Additional revenues were secured by levies upon public utilities, coal and iron operators, and tobacco, and by doubling the franchise tax of all corporations. Grover C. Hall, editor of the Montgomery *Advertiser*, later summed it up with the comment that "Bibb Graves makes a good governor, but an expensive one."

A striking contrast to the dynamic "little Colonel," "Bibb the Builder," was Austin Peay, governor of Tennessee from 1923 to 1927. A small town lawyer from Clarksville who had served in the legislature, the epitome of colorlessness, he announced for governor in 1922, leaving to others "any pleasure of fine periods in the campaign," and confining himself "to bare facts and statistics, with which my mind is accustomed to deal."

After the fashion of business-progressive rhetoric, he called for a "clean, honest and courageous Legislature, working under sane direction to repeal laws and reduce government in Tennessee." Carried to victory in the Democratic primary, he defeated Alfred Taylor, Republican governor of the state, in the general election. Alf Taylor cracked jokes and told stories about his dog, "Old Limber." Peay stuck to his statistics and his paradoxical exposition of the state's need for tax reform, reduced expenditures, highways, and schools.

Swept into office with a comfortable majority, Peay summoned expert assistance at his own expense to develop a reorganization bill that regrouped sixty-four scattered agencies under eight commissioners directly responsible to the governor. The resulting efficiency, it was claimed, saved the state over a million dollars in two years. The state tax system was overhauled, with reductions in land taxes but a new privilege tax on corporate earnings, a gasoline tax for highways, and a tobacco tax for an eight-month school term in rural schools. Despite his appeal for the reduction of government, Peay directed an expansion of the road system and public schools that cost far more than the savings from his reorganization plan. By 1929 Tennessee had developed 5,000 miles of surfaced roads in its state system, in contrast to about 500 in 1920, and all but thirteen of its ninety-five counties had an eight-month school term in contrast to fewer than one-third with more than five months in 1920.

The reluctant progressive may be typified by the young Harry Flood Byrd, governor of Virginia, 1926–1930, whose strong points were efficiency and the promotion of industry. An F.F.V., newspaper publisher, apple-grower, a self-made businessman, heir to the old "machine," Byrd, in one revealing address, compared government to business: the governor as president of the corporation, the legislature as board of directors, the taxpayers as stockholders, the dividends paid in public services. "The administration of government," he said, "should be efficiently conducted along the lines of well organized business enterprises, but the benefits of government cannot be measured by the yardstick of the dollar. The cost . . . has enormously increased . . . and the need of improved efficiency becomes daily more important." However, once made efficient, a state government should not extend beyond the discharge of functions "public necessities have imposed on it"; "undue extension" of government activities should be avoided.

True to his philosophy, Byrd, like Peay, carried through an extensive reorganization. More than one hundred bureaus, boards, and commissions were integrated into fourteen departments and a short ballot was inaugurated. These reforms, Byrd wrote, were "progressive and modern, and yet they were approved by popular vote in one of the oldest and most conservative of the states." Tax reform included the segregation of land taxes to local uses and the reduction of taxes on capital investments, and Governor Byrd personally embarked on a campaign to attract industries to the state. But even Byrd, whose watchword was economy above all, was carried along by the highway campaign of the twenties. Opponent of a state bond issue in 1923, which was defeated by a popular majority, he turned in his campaign to support of a pay-as-you-go system and championed generous tax increases that made possible annual state expenditures of fourteen million dollars on highways and nearly 5,000 miles of surfaced roads in the state system by 1929.

In other states business-progressive governors and programs enjoyed greater or lesser success. The slogan of Arkansas' Governor John E. Martineau, "Better Roads and Better Schools," could stand almost as a motto for the decade, although in Arkansas failure to rationalize state government and the development of roads through a proliferation of uncoordinated local districts led the state finally to assume heavy debts that bankrupted it in the Depression. In some states progressive governors were unable to get the support of legislatures for their programs: Pat Neff and Dan Moody in Texas, for example, and Lamartine G. Hardman in Georgia. In Kentucky suspicious voters decisively rejected in 1924 a bond issue of $75,000,000 which was to be spent chiefly for highways and schools. In other states there was no strong central figure in the development of policies, but everywhere efficiency and expansion were central themes in state politics. South Carolina politics, a state historian wrote, experienced an era of "vacuity," but the state started the decade with the lowest public school expenditure per pupil in the country and ended it with the highest rate of increase. It climaxed the decade with a $65,000,000 highway bond issue in 1929. In Florida the land boom provided resources for the expansion of services.

State after state took up administrative and tax reforms, and despite much pious talk about economy, state and local governments were undertaking ambitious programs on every hand. Every southern state adopted some kind of budget system between 1918 and

1928, and several went through general reorganizations while similar programs were advanced or partially adopted in all. The expansion of state services, battening on industrial prosperity and optimism, moved along at an accelerated pace.

The rate of increase in both state revenues and debt in the South far exceeded that for the rest of the nation. The search for revenue led to a variety of new taxes. Gasoline taxes, nonexistent before 1919, produced some $129,000,000 for southern states in 1929, about one-third of their revenues. Motor vehicle registrations produced receipts of $54,299,442 in 1933. By 1929 eight southern states in a total of twenty-one had adopted the income tax, and revenues from that source rose 137 percent between 1923 and 1928. Of nine states having a sales tax in 1932, five were southeastern; nine of thirteen had cigarette and tobacco taxes. The revenues of local government meanwhile were increased by the rise in property assessments and by the tendency to apply property taxes to local purposes.

There can be no question that the South more than any other region was straining its resources for the support and expansion of public services. In both the ratio of tax collections to aggregate private income and in per capita state indebtedness, the region ranked ahead of all others by 1930. And yet the old story of relative poverty remained. In spite of enormous increases the South still lagged behind in actual revenues. In actual per capita collections in 1930, nine southern states were at the bottom of the list and eleven in the lowest quartile. Florida, the highest, ranked only eighteenth in the nation. In 1932 the general revenues of state and local governments in the thirteen southern states amounted to $33.26 per capita, less than half the $69.63 per capita for the non-South.

In the development of state government, a student of Tennessee finances has claimed, three main stages may be identified down to 1929. The first, until 1904, was the "debt" period, during which debt service outranked other expenditures; this was followed by a period of increasing expenditures for schools until about 1921; while expenditures for schools continued to rise after that, the twenties were overwhelmingly dominated by highways. This was characteristic of other states. "Good roads," Francis B. Simkins wrote, "became the third god in the trinity of Southern progress"—after industry and education. In all the southern states by 1930 highways and education far outdistanced other state functions. In none were expenditures for the two functions less than 60 percent of state expenditures, and in only three, less than 70. Some idea of the priorities of business progressivism, however, may be derived from the fact that in all but the three same states, the state expenditures for highways were greater than those for education.

The story of the good-roads movement still awaits its historian. As yet there is scarcely any monographic literature tracing its development. It is a diffuse story, of conventions and associations, bicyclists and motorists, the promotion of name highways by aggregations of local promoters, of "heroic caravans in dusters and goggles," and finally broad-gauged planning of integrated programs with the federal highways acts of 1916 and 1921 and the development of state systems. In any case, it is clear from the results that the movement had won general support by the twenties. Expenditures for the construction of state-administered highway systems increased by 157 percent in the South during the twenties (1920–1929) and 123 percent outside the South.

For education as for roads, the twenties were years of emergence from the phase of crusading into an era of efficiency and expansion. School busses increasingly moved across improved highways to new consolidated schools. The foundations in the field, led by the great central directorate of the General Education Board, still did a tremendous job of promoting schools. But gradually state and local governments were taking over the programs the foundations had inaugurated: agents for rural secondary and Negro schools; surveys and studies of educational needs; special administrative divisions for the systematic collection of information, schoolhouse planning and construction, the promotion of libraries, developing standards of teacher training and certification. And, if the average cost per pupil in every southern state was still in 1930 well below the national average, eight southern states since 1920 had exceeded the national rate of increase in cost per pupil. Nine had exceeded the national rate of increase in length of school term, although none reached the national average length of school term, with the exception of Oklahoma.

Concentration upon schools and highways, however, should not obscure the fact that the state and local governments were moving ahead in other public services, if on a more restricted scale. Beginning with North Carolina in 1917, every southern state except Mississippi had established by 1927 some kind of state system of public welfare. By 1930 welfare expenditures amounted to 3.8 percent of total governmental costs in the Southeast and 4.2 percent in the Southwest.

A much more rapid growth was the development of public health programs under the impact of successive crusades for the conquest of tuberculosis, hookworm, malaria, pellagra, and syphilis. The result was a rapid development of county health departments to carry the word and the cures to the people on a continuing basis. In eleven southeastern states county health departments increased from 94 in 1920 to 166 in 1925 to 347 in 1930, the latter constituting nearly 63 percent of the departments in the nation.

A rough measure of the full scope of governmental expansion might be derived from reference to the state handbooks prepared for the legislatures. The North Carolina manuals indicate that state administrative departments, boards, and commissions increased from twelve in 1913 to twenty in 1921 to sixty in 1929, and state educational, charitable, and correctional institutions from eighteen to twenty-one to thirty-two. New functions represented by the new agencies in the twenties included conservation, promotion of industry, new budgetary and fiscal programs, child welfare, the licensing of various professions, a state bureau of investigation, and new penal and correctional institutions.

What happened to southern governments in the twenties was not unrelated to what happened in other fields. It was a period of emergence, in which numerous forces began to reach fruition. If what W. J. Cash called the savage ideal of intolerance and repression seemed to have achieved a new ferocity in the Klan and the fundamentalists, it may be suggested that it was the ferocity of those who found themselves in a losing battle against broadening horizons. If it was the period of the Klan and fundamentalism, it was also the period of economic emergence, the interracial movement, the renaissance in literature, the rise of universities which inspired critical analysis of southern problems. In the very same column quoted at the beginning of this essay, Mencken noted that "Odums hatch out day by day all over the late Confederacy. The very heat of the fundamentalist and Ku Klux fury is hurrying them out of the egg."

Meanwhile, the Atlanta spirit had caught up the governments of the South, as well as its businessmen, in a zeal for the New South Triumphant. The business-progressive philosophy, to be sure, had its limitations. Race relations were assumed to be a settled problem. The larger economic problems of the underprivileged, farm tenants and factory workers, were not its problems; their remedy would come, if at all, through economic expansion. In turn, business progressivism created new problems: the political influence of the new agencies, the highway departments, the road contractors, the trucking lobbies, the teachers' associations; and soon, in the Depression, the debts came due with severe repercussions on the extended state and local governments. Expansion of state activities required a pressure and strain to accomplish what was a matter of course in wealthier states. But the continuing development of public services in the twenties was at least a partial confirmation of the old maxim that yesterday's radicalism is today's moderation. Deep forces flowed through the period, forces that originated before the twenties and issued into later decades. The business-progressive philosophy had deep roots in both the progressive movement and the "New South" creed of economic

development. It was severely shaken by the Depression
and the New Deal, but the progressivism of expansion
and efficiency became by and large the norm of southern statecraft in the decades that followed.

8

Populism:
A Semantic Identity Crisis

DURING THE 1972 CAMPAIGN THE CASUAL READER MUST have had the impression that the country harbored more Populists per square mile than at any time since 1896. In the capricious world of political high fashion, the "new populism" was for a season all the go, the biggest thing since radical chic. Now the pundits are off to pastures new and the historians can get back to the real thing. But it will not be easy. We can hardly avoid confusion when we remember that the rubric *populism* covered everybody from Spiro Agnew to Bella Abzug or from George Wallace to George McGovern. And what is one to make of that "band of populist sinners and dancers" who, according to *Time*, gyrated through Leonard Bernstein's *Mass*? Or those "populist portfolio managers" to whom, according to *Newsweek*, investors were turning. We may well doubt that many real populists were ever found in the concert hall or on Wall Street. The party of course did harbor a few termagants who might pep up the fem lib movements today, but even they would no doubt be mystified by *Ms.* magazine and its monthly column of homely advice on "Populist Mechanics."

As early as August, 1971, we could read in the New York *Times* that a "New Populism" had erupted in Mississippi and that the National Student Association, an important touchstone of the prevailing taste, had discarded anarchism in favor of populism. Then *Time*, which is more intoxicated with the word than most journals, discovered that the people of Montana "brew 100-proof populism and partake of it as effortlessly as they drink their bourbon." A convention in Helena compiled in 1972 what may be the first populistic state constitution in history.

Clearly David Halberstam was too quick to label Albert Gore "the last populist" and obviously those writers who used to pin the same label on Wright Patman were in error. From sundry sources one gathers that the populists currently number, among others, Reubin Askew, Dale Bumpers, Jimmy Carter, Lawton Chiles, Edwin Edwards, Sam Ervin, Henry E. Howell, Harold Hughes, Lester Maddox, Wilbur Mills, Dan Walker, and, *mirabile dictu*, John D. Rockefeller IV. According to Anthony Lewis of the New York *Times*, Lyndon Johnson was "beyond doubt a genuine populist"—certainly his grandfather was. The first self-confessed populist candidate for president in 1972, Fred R. Harris, offered some proof that *he* was the genuine article by running out of money. He was followed by, among others, Henry "Scoop" Jackson, known to *Ramparts* as a "Pentagon Populist," and Hubert Humphrey, who styled himself "The People's Democrat," explaining that the slogan meant he was and always had been a Populist. During the primaries candidates even took to denouncing each other as "phony populists." The front runner for that title was George C. Wallace, also known to *Newsweek* as a "populist cum segregationist." Finally we got as the Democratic candidate George S. McGovern, the celebrated "prairie populist," who personally avoided using the label, however.

It seemed at first that only a Democrat could qualify any more. Then a reporter discovered that Congressman "Vinegar Bend" Mizell (North Carolina Republican) was a populist—because he opposed construction of a dam on New River—and others detected overtones of populism in the rabble-rousing of Spiro Agnew. One thing, at least, seemed dependable: in keeping with their parochial heritage populists flourished mainly in the South, to some extent in the West, and hardly at all in the East, certainly not in the metropolis. Then we learned that John Lindsay had switched parties in order to lead the forces of "urban populism" and *Time* discovered that Bella Abzug was a "female populist." And suddenly a new People's party surfaced, running Dr. Benjamin Spock for president.

What, the reader begins to wonder, can all this gallimaufry have in common with hayseed rebels like "Whiskers" Peffer, Ignatius Donnelly, and Tom Watson? Could we possibly envision John Lindsay as a modern Sockless Jerry Simpson damning his adversaries for wearing silk stockings? Or what is slightly more incredible, Bella Abzug as a latter-day Mary Elizabeth Lease exhorting the rustics of Manhattan to raise, if not less corn, at least less porn and, in any case, more hell? Do our living populists champion free silver, the subtreasury plan, public ownership of railroads, or postal savings banks? Do they find a natural harmony of interests among the "producing classes" as against the "parasites"? Is the whole connection less a matter of program than of style—or is it something else again?

Perhaps we should begin the search for clues in the history of the original Populists. The People's party, which climaxed a generation of farmer discontent, flourished mainly in the years from 1890 to 1896. The movement sprang chiefly from the rural South and West and derived from deep-seated grievances caused by the decay of the farmer's economic condition. Populism won few elections but it fulfilled what has been the historic function of third parties in American politics. It gave voice to discontent. It advanced new issues and it forced the major parties to take them up.

The Populist platform of 1892 was almost a checklist of reforms to come. It called for currency inflation, farm credit, a graduated income tax, and postal savings banks. Other planks demanded governmental ownership of railroads and the reservation of public lands for actual settlers. Political and economic demands included the secret ballot, the initiative and referendum, popular election of senators, a single term for president and vice-president, and—in a gesture toward urban workers —the eight-hour day and restriction of immigration. Condemnations of the tariff and of subsidies to corporations rounded out the platform.

In 1892 presidential candidate James B. Weaver of Iowa polled better than a million popular votes and twenty-two electoral votes on the Populist ticket. A severe depression after the Panic of 1893 seemed to destine the Populists for major-party status, but in the next three years President Cleveland's effort to save the gold standard focused attention more and more on the currency. In 1896 William Jennings Bryan preempted the silver issue and ran off with both the Democratic and Populist nominations. The Populists, amid recriminations over Bryan's refusal to accept their vice-presidential candidate, Thomas E. Watson of Georgia, went down in the general defeat of Bryan.

After 1896 farm prices improved and the People's party collapsed. The focus of the reform spirit shifted to the cities, where middle-class progressives attacked the problems of urban development, political bossism, and industrial monopoly. The precise relationship of populism and progressivism is still a subject of controversy among historians, but during the years down to World War I, an amalgam of rural and urban reformers produced a body of legislation that fulfilled much of the Populist program, and more besides. There was little question among the adherents of populism, and some of its adversaries, that populism achieved vindication in the progressive era. William Allen White of Emporia, Kansas, who first achieved fame with a widely copied editorial against populism, eventually reversed his opinion. Populism, he wrote later, "was the beginning of a movement that in another decade was to change the politics of the nation; indeed it was a symptom of a world wide drift to liberalism, which reached its peak in Christendom twenty-five years later."

For half a century historians of populism put the movement in the broad tradition of American liberalism. In 1931 John D. Hicks published his monumental study, *The Populist Revolt*, which stood for years as the definitive work and remains the indispensable starting point for investigation of the movement. In that book the Populists emerged as a group clearly in the reform tradition, the heirs of Jacksonian democracy and the precursors of progressivism.

Throughout the twenty years of the New and Fair Deals, the Populists remained in good odor among those intellectuals who embraced the neo-Populist farmer-labor-liberal coalition of Franklin D. Roosevelt. Their euphoric identification with the Populist heritage prevailed into the 1950s. Then, in 1955, historian Richard Hofstadter handed up a startling indictment. The Populists, he charged in *The Age of Reform: From Bryan to F. D. R.*, had sought scapegoats more than solutions, had suffered paranoid delusions of conspiracy by the money power, had fostered anti-Semitism, xenophobia, jingoism, parochialism, and feverish visions of cataclysm. Populist thinking, Hofstadter suggested, "has survived in our own time, partly as an undercurrent of popular resentments, popular and 'democratic' rebelliousness and suspiciousness, and nativism."

For several years the musty documents of populism furnished ammunition for one of the most spirited battles in American historiography. Other writers, less careful than Hofstadter, and less steeped in history, located in populism the fountainhead of American fascism, the radical right, anti-intellectualism, McCarthyism, witch-hunting, and other malignities. Such writers, however, revealed more about the anxieties of urban intellectuals in the 1950s than about populism in the 1890s. Behind their treatment of populism, the sinister figure of Joseph McCarthy lurked against a backdrop of loyalty oaths and witch-hunts. Intellectuals had discovered the seamy side of democracy, and by some kind of spontaneous combustion they hit upon the name *populism* as the modern equivalent for an outmoded word, *mobocracy*. "Populism has many faces," political scientist Edward Shils wrote. "Nazi dictatorship had markedly populistic features. . . . Bolshevism had a strand of populism in it too." According to the poet and publicist Peter Viereck, populistic attitudes "underlay Robespierre's Committee of Public Safety" and later "our neo-Populist Committee on un-American activities."

Hofstadter had focused on the historic Populists and had carefully qualified his arguments. He admitted to rigging the scales in order to rectify the balance, and one can no longer evaluate populism without weighing certain components that earlier historians neglected. Yet one need not conclude that populism bore a unique burden of those elements or that it was a supreme force in their dissemination.

Insofar as the critics of populism were reading back into the 1890s the anxieties of the 1950s, their argument has been pretty much exploded by subsequent studies. C. Vann Woodward's essay, "The Populist Heritage and the Intellectual" (1959), suggested most of the counterarguments and admonished intellectuals against repudiating the heritage of movements which, as he put it, "shock the seats of power and privilege and furnish the periodic therapy that seems necessary to the health of our democracy." Walter T. K. Nugent's book, *The Tolerant Populists: Kansas Populism and Nativism* (1963) showed the Populists, in Kansas at least, as rather less narrow-minded than their neighbors. Michael Rogin's *The Intellectuals and McCarthy* (1967) not only shattered the notion that Joseph McCarthy was heir to populism but advanced a telling critique of theorists who interpret "efforts by masses to improve their condition as threats to stability" and turn "all threats to stability into threats to constitutional democracy." In *The Populist Response to Industrial America* (1962), Norman Pollack may have overplayed his hand, but in that book he went so far as to make the Populists out as pretty sophisticated political theorists.

Still, during the 1950s the Populist image acquired a certain tarnish. Now it seems to be regaining its luster. Having been for more than a decade a pejorative epithet for vulgar prejudice, *populism* now crops up as a term of praise for broad compassion. Anthony Lewis, for instance, elaborating in the New York *Times* on the meaning of "genuine populist," called Lyndon Johnson after all "a man who cared about the poor and rejected in society, an egalitarian reformer."

Here, perhaps, the dawn begins to glimmer. Despite suspicions that the Populist farmers qualified as petty capitalists who wanted above all a return on their property, the notion persists (with good reason) that they did care about the poor and rejected. But so, by common report, have many Christians, reformers, progressives, radicals, New Dealers, utopians, and assorted do-gooders. Few candidates for public office would deny the charge. So why "populists"?

Can the current mutation be simply a throwback to the Latin root of the word: *populus*, meaning people? A similar word appeared in ancient Rome, where patrician leaders who cultivated the plebeian masses were called *populares*, the greatest of whom was Julius Caesar. The word *Populist* did not appear in standard English dictionaries down to 1890, but it was in circulation by 1891. Contemporary evidence of its origin has yet to be uncovered, but later accounts from several sources credited its invention to David Overmyer, a Kansas Democrat. Sometime during 1890 (or perhaps 1891), aboard a Santa Fe train from Kansas City to Topeka, Overmyer fell into conversation with W. F. Rightmire, a leader of the Kansas People's party, who remarked that members of his party needed a shorter name like Democrat or Republican, and from his memory of Latin, Overmyer brought forth the word *Populist*. Two journalists who were involved in the conversation put the word in circulation within a week.

All the older dictionaries capitalized *Populist* and associated it with the People's party. Dictionaries persist in capitalizing it, for the most part, but *Webster's Third International* now admits another definition: "a member of a political party purporting to represent the rank and file of the people." This would seem to cover a lot of political parties.

The *Third International*, however, omits still another definition which appears in the *Oxford English Dictionary*: "A member of a Russian socio-political party advocating a form of collectivism." The word is here applied, a bit too narrowly, to something entirely different from American populism. The Russian word *narodnichestvo* derives from *narod*, meaning people, and therefore by a semantic accident (but literal analogy) is commonly translated as *populism*. The standard work on the movement was first published in Italian, under the title, *Il Popolismo Russo*. In English it is *Roots of Revolution*. *Narodnichestvo* entered the Russian vocabulary sometime during the 1870s to designate the ideas of certain intellectuals who proposed "going to the people" or "learning from the people," or who at least idealized the people as the fountainhead of national virtue. Unlike American populism it was chiefly a movement of intellectuals, some of whom in their naïve efforts to work among the muzhiks foretokened American "student revolutionaries" of recent years going out to the workers. It was an early case of radical chic, the more bizarre aspects of which were the objects of Feodor Dostoevsky's censure in his novel, *The Possessed*, which was a satire on fanaticism. At the end of the 1870s some of the most radical of "the possessed" formed a terrorist group called People's Will, the activities of which reached their climax with the assassination of Czar Alexander II in 1881.

In common usage, however, *narodnichestvo* embraced a broad spectrum of opinion, from liberal-democratic to socialist-revolutionary, from the pacifist Leo Tolstoy to the terrorist Sergei Nechaev. The usage became so confusing that A. N. Pypin, a Russian literary historian, wrote in 1884 a complaint that might have been written by an American today: "'Narodnichestvo' which one hears so often mentioned these days is something extremely unclear, difficult to define, and arbitrary. 'Narodniki' is used by and for people who have very little in common, and often bear no resemblance to each other: people with very progressive opinions, or people who, while they assert with every breath that they are special friends of the people, preach something very close to obscurantism."

But Pypin himself adopted the word and gave it a broad cultural definition. In his usage *narodnichestvo* covered a concern with and respect for the common heritage of the masses: ethnography, folklore, the history of language, and popular culture. This notion seems to owe something to the late eighteenth-century romantic German philosopher and historian, Johann Gottfried Herder. And we have it on no less authority than Sir Isaiah Berlin that Herder was a populist, although he could not possibly have known it. Indeed to this day the word has not entered the German language. German historians have avoided semantic confusion by simply using the American or Russian word, whichever is appropriate.

Berlin, writing in *Encounter*, defines populism as "the belief in the value of belonging to a group or culture, which, for Herder at least, is not political, and is indeed, to some degree, anti-political." It was Herder who developed the notion of *Volksgeist*, or spirit of the folk, in reaction against the universalism of the Enlightened *philosophes*. This idea, said Berlin, was "at the heart of all populism."

In Russia, however, the word continued to have a political application, for *narodnichestvo* was a vast current of thought that nourished the seedbeds of revolution. Many of the later Marxists were once *narodniki*, and even Lenin drew some of his ideas from them; yet the word somehow became a malediction among the Marxists. During the 1890s it was applied to a faction of the Social Democrats who took the unorthodox position that Russia could bypass the bourgeois-capitalist stage of development and move directly to socialism. In this usage the *narodniki* were typed as hopelessly utopian and Slavophile, and the word became a polemical device to establish Marxism as a new and triumphant movement, superseding all the previous *narodniki* movements.

Among the historians of Russia there is disagreement about this interpretation, but, in any case, *narodnichestvo* remained a scandal throughout the Stalin era. We need not sink any further into the morass of Russian populism and variant usages of the word, however, to detect some curious parallels to the history of our own word. A word that in its origins meant some kind of vaguely democratic or socialist reform became a hissing and a reproach. The parallel carries even further. By recent reports the word is regaining its luster. Soviet historians are once again giving sympathetic attention to their heritage of populism.

The quest for the meaning of populism would remain a reasonably simple task if it were just a matter of sorting out nineteenth-century movements in the Bible and Balalaika Belts. But in the last decade or so the social scientists of the world have mounted the hobby horse of "populism" and ridden off rapidly in all directions. A glance at the 1968 edition of the *International Encyclopedia of the Social Sciences* will suggest the magnitude of their new departure. In the original *Encyclopedia* (1933) the index shows only two mentions of "populism": one in reference to the People's party and another in reference to an attitude of faith in the people. In the later edition, however, populism has become a protean monster.

In an essay on "Intellectuals," for instance, Edward Shils writes: "Populism, which is partly an offspring of the romantic tradition, is a belief in the creativity and and superior moral worth of the ordinary people, of the uneducated and unintellectual." In an essay on "Mass

Society," sociologist William Kornhauser says: "Mass equalitarianism is expressed in the populist character of mass society. . . . Political régimes strive to be popular régimes, whether they are dictatorial or constitutional. While this popular legitimation of authority centers in the polity, it pervades all kinds of social institutions." Elsewhere, in his book *The Politics of Mass Society*, Kornhauser asserts: "The uniformity of opinion among large numbers of people becomes the supreme standard, superordinate to traditional values, professional standards, and institutional autonomy." This, too, is "populism."

In Egon Bittner's article on "Radicalism," American populism is traced "back to the ideals of Jeffersonian democracy," elements of which "in the hands of Jackson became a permanent radical trend in American politics." Bittner mentions the Russian version and adds the German Romantics, beginning with Herder, who devoted themselves to folklore, ethnic history, and glorification of the *Volk*. And if we return to Edward Shil's article on "Intellectuals," we are abruptly off on a world tour: "in Brazil (in the doctrine of 'Indianismo'), in the resentful and embittered aesthetic 'left' and romantic 'right' of the Weimar Republic, in India since the ascendancy of Ghandi, and in the emerging intellectual strata of the new countries of Africa, populistic tendencies have been massively at work." We are suddenly far away from Kansas—or Kazan.

Just how far was demonstrated in the essays submitted to an international conference of scholars at the London School of Economics in 1967, published in 1969 under the title, *Populism: Its Meanings and National Characteristics*, edited by Ghita Ionescu and Ernest Gellner. Here we find that the word has been picked up as a rubric for diverse movements of the "Third World." Thus, in Latin America we find references to five major varieties of *populismo*: multiclass integrative parties, like Mexico's PRI; *Aprista* parties, like Peru's; Nasserist, or military reforming parties (*El Populismo Militar* is the title of a pamphlet published at Lima in 1969!); social revolutionary parties (Castroist); and Peronist parties. It is mainly an urban phenomenon, especially in Brazil. In eastern Europe there have been a number of peasant movements, or élite movements glorifying the peasants, all more or less indebted to Russian populism for their rationale. In Africa the term refers to the idea of *négritude*, to a "growing popular participation and awakened popular consciousness in recent African history," to a critique of capitalism, to political rallying cries for solidarity, to the attitude of anxious intellectuals who "praise the culture of the ordinary man as richer, truer, wiser, and more relevant than the foreign culture in which they themselves had been educated."

In one essay, "A Syndrome, Not a Doctrine," Peter Wiles of the London School of Economics attempts a partial list of people and movements who may be called populist. His populist pantheon includes the Levellers, Diggers, and Chartists of England; the narodniki and Socialist Revolutionaries of Russia; the American Populists; Gandhi in India; Sinn Fein in Ireland; the Iron Guard in Rumania; Social Credit in Alberta and the Cooperative Commonwealth Federation in Saskatchewan; Cárdenas in Mexico; Haya de la Torre and Belaúnde Terry in Peru; Poujade in France; Nyerere in Tanzania. Professor Wiles confesses that his list is incomplete. He misses, among other distinguished populists, Adolf Hitler, Mao Tse-tung, Fidel Castro, Frantz Fanon, and Father Coughlin.

A startling variation on Marx and Engels opened the report from the London conference: "A spectre is haunting the world—populism." It may be that the spectre is haunting chiefly the social scientists of the world, who are up to an old trick of latching onto new jargon. Yet one must acknowledge the possibility that all this smoke might indicate a fire somewhere. The new usages of *populism* may turn out to have a value as a conceptual paradigm (to use another vogue-word), however murky the resolution of the problem may seem at the moment, and however much one might wish for a word less loaded with historical connotation and semantic confusion. Five of the ten essays submitted to the conference address the problem of definitions. One of them, especially, suggests a certain promise of clarification: "The Social Roots," by Angus Stewart of the London School of Economics.

The unity of populism, Stewart argues, lies not in the content of programs but in the similarity of situations. The various movements gathered under the umbrella of populism have appeared, he argues, "in societies and social groups which . . . have become aware of being peripheral to centres of power." Associated with this are problems of eroded legitimacy. "Populistic mobilization represents attempts to revitalize integration on the basis of 'traditional' values." Also, populism equates the nation and the people; virtue dwells in the simple folk.

Populism, Stewart writes, responds to a crisis of development: mainly the decision to industrialize and how, and the consequences thereof. Russian populism, for instance, responded to the former; American populism to the latter. Populism has a Janus quality. On one side it looks back to a golden age or idealizes some tradition. On the other side it seeks to modernize. Thus it fosters an ideology which seeks to organize social reconstruction around traditional institutions of the people: the American small farm, the Russian *mir*, the Mexican *ejido*, the African village. Both left- and right-wing variants tend to extol the virtues of rural life and attack the vices of the city, and frequently fall into delusions of hostile conspiracies, either by some imperialist power or by a native establishment.

A definition offered by another of the essayists, Kenneth Minogue, seems to identify one central feature that is present in all the variant movements: "a collective awareness of disadvantage in relation to wealth; and in a modern context, wealth happens to mean industrial power. The point about the location of populist movements is not that they are rural but that they are peripheral to economic power."

Before returning from this excursion through space and time, we need to pause at one more exotic port of call. The Greeks had a word for it, too. Just as the Americans and Russians derived their terms from words meaning *people*, the Greeks derived from their word *demos* the word *demagogos*. In Greek it meant literally and simply "leader of the people," but in English *demagogue* long ago acquired the associations of passion and prejudice which we now attach to it, and which some attach to the word *populist* as well.

More than that, the words have a demonstrable connection in our history, a connection that was curiously

slighted by writers who tried to get up a populistic genealogy for Joe McCarthy. Unlike McCarthy, the classic
"southern demagogues" did stem in a direct line from
the likes of Tom Watson, who stands as the prototype
of the Populist who turned sour. Once the leader of an
interracial coalition, Watson later sought the disfranchisement of Negroes, launched scurrilous attacks on
Catholics and Jews, and contributed indirectly to the
resurrection of the Ku Klux Klan. His successors right
on down to George Wallace have combined elements of
populism and demagoguery in a clotted mixture.

After the farmers' movement of the 1890s had undermined the deference of plebeians to their betters, "redneck" revolts erupted wherever artful leaders arose to
exploit the frustrations of poverty and ignorance: James
K. Vardaman and Theodore G. Bilbo in Mississippi,
Jeff Davis in Arkansas, James and Miriam or "Pa" and
"Ma" Ferguson in Texas, Cole Blease in South Carolina,
Huey Long in Louisiana, Eugene Talmadge in Georgia
—to name a few. They offered, if nothing else, a kind
of catharsis and vicarious fulfillment for their followers,
and sometimes they offered more substantial rewards.
But this comes precariously close to calling them people
who cared about the poor and rejected in society.

Confusion is worse confounded when we remember
that most of the demagogues exploited resentments of
white against black, although the Populists seldom did.
On the contrary their "producer rhetoric" provided the
rationale for a political unity that rose above race. "You
are kept apart that you may be separately fleeced of
your earnings," the earlier Tom Watson said. "You are
deceived and blinded that you may not see how this
race antagonism perpetuates a monetary system which

beggars both." The extent and depth of the temporary
interracial unity inspired by populism may be easily
exaggerated. Given more time the movement might
have penetrated the color line significantly, but it hardly
lasted long enough and was followed by a reaction that
entrenched race antagonism all the more. Yet the memory of that coalition has been repeatedly renewed and
romanticized. Any sign of interracial cooperation is
likely to be hailed as a harbinger of neopopulism.

In the last two decades the word has acquired a dual
quality: yin and yang, Jekyll and Hyde, progressivism
and paranoia. Recently three political scientists, focus-
ing on the American scene, tackled the problem with
an article, "In Search of Populism," by James Clotfelter,
William Hamilton, and Peter Harkins, which appeared
in *New South*, a publication of the Southern Regional
Council. Unlike some of our hurried journalists, the
authors of this article acknowledge the "vagueness of
the populist notion" which "stems partly from the inconsistencies of historical American populism." Still, they
seem persuaded that there is something out there called
populism, waiting only to be discovered. Their definition, however, is grounded mostly in examples of hostility that turn up in polling-samples of white southerners.

For them populist attitudes include support for social
welfare measures (unless they are linked to blacks or
taxes), endorsement of "populist-flavored 'alienation' or
'cynicism' statements" ("It's still hard for the average
man to get a fair shake"), and making scapegoats of
groups perceived as threatening (a mixed bag of sub-
versives, deadbeats, liberals, intellectuals, big corporations, and, above all, blacks). Populism encompasses

"groups below the median in social class or income, but not usually including the poor and the destitute— in short, Middle America and the silent majority.

In that essay populism seems to be an assortment of ill-focused discontents and prejudices, which one can hardly separate from the old demagoguery. Yet the tone of the article and the context of wider usage hold out the hope that what has come to be called the "new populism" promises something positive and beneficent. Twentieth-century populism (whatever it is) has yet to produce a polemical literature of economic, social, and political analysis remotely comparable to that of the farmers' movement, but the current vogue of the word suggests a certain potential as the rallying cry for a new departure in American politics.

The presidential year 1972 saw the appearance of two manifestoes of the new populism. The first, *Now is the Time: A Populist Call to Action* was by Fred R. Harris. Senator Harris at least offered a definite program under the rubric of *populism*: decent incomes, more social security, health care, and trustbusting. It sounded almost like old times down home. Harris, moreover, reached beyond Middle America to champion an alliance of poor whites and blacks, and even beyond the old populism to include Chicanos, Indians, and other minorities.

But Harris, the son of an Oklahoma tenant farmer, was soon challenged as the chief guru of populism by two rather unlikely candidates: Jack Newfield, associate editor of the *Village Voice*, who earlier chronicled the rise of SDS, and Jeff Greenfield, a graduate of Yale Law School and former speechwriter for Robert F. Kennedy. The contribution of "Newgreenfield," as one reviewer labeled them, is *A Populist Manifesto: The Making of a New Majority*, which has far more detailed and specific proposals than Harris' book. The core of their manifesto, they write, "lies in this perception: there are people, classes, and institutions that today possess an illegitimate amount of wealth and power; they use that power for their own benefit and for the common loss. This power, which is at root economic, corrupts the political process and insulates itself from effective challenge." The rhetoric faithfully echoes Ignatius Donnelly's preamble to the Populist platform of 1892: "We meet in the midst of a nation brought to the verge of moral, political and material ruin. . . . The fruits of the toil of millions are boldly stolen to build up colossal fortunes for a few, unprecedented in the history of mankind."

The specifics, however, go far beyond those of 1892; they carry echoes of progressivism and the New Deal plus much that is newer. Like Harris, "Newgreenfield" propose better incomes, social security, health care, and trustbusting, but they add detailed proposals for reforming the tax structure, regulating banks and insurance companies, revitalizing the Federal Trade Commission and other regulatory agencies, nationalizing utilities, distributing land, controlling crime, reforming labor unions, and bringing foreign policy and the political process in general under more democratic control. The new majority they envision would mobilize youth, the aged, consumer advocates, ecologists, ethnic workers, blacks, farmers, and the aggrieved masses in general.

Whether we are witness to the birth of a new political

movement or simply present at the birth of a new breed, the parlor populist, we are clearly seeing a process of evolution in language. The problem is one to which Francis Bacon testified in his *Novum Organum* more than three centuries ago: "For men believe that their reason governs words, but it is also true that words react on the understanding. . . . Whence it comes to pass that the high and formal discussions of learned men end oftentimes in disputes about words and names with which . . . it would be more prudent to begin, and so by means of definitions reduce them to order." *Populism*, of course, is not the first political term to acquire variant definitions, which tend to be frayed at the edges. One need only think of such terms as *democracy, socialism, liberalism*, and *conservatism*.

The variant meanings of *populism* aside from its historical reference to quite different movements in the United States and Russia, may be summarized as follows. First, the term may refer to a celebration of the *Volksgeist*, as with Herder and assorted folklorists, ethnographers, and nationalists who have found virtue in the qualities or potentialities of ordinary people. Second, it may refer to theories of the popular will and may suggest the tyranny of the majority, the spirit of popular conformity that so impressed de Tocqueville in nineteenth-century America. Third, *populism* has become a conceptual paradigm for sociologists and political scientists who apply it to all sorts of popular movements, especially in the "Third World." Fourth, it has emerged as the rallying cry for a new political movement in the United States: the new populism. And fifth, it is currently a vogue-word among journalists for any figure or phenomenon which appeals to the masses of the people.

Until these variations have been resolved better than they have been so far—or rejected in favor of greater precision—the publicists and politicians might take a leaf from the books of Harris, Newfield, and Greenfield, and explain, when they use the word *populism*, exactly what they want it to mean. Until they do, we may have to fall back on the definition offered by my friend and colleague Louis Rubin: "A populist is a rabblerouser you like. If you don't like him, he's a demagogue."

9

The Bubble in the Sun

THE IMPULSE THAT CARRIED THEYRE HAMILTON WEI-
gall into the Miami madness of 1925 was about as logical
as that which carried anybody else into it. An unem-
ployed English newspaperman wandering the streets of
New York in the summer of that year, he was suddenly
stopped by a sign in a window announcing that there
were fortunes to be made in Florida real estate. "One
Good Investment Beats a Lifetime of Toil. Say! YOU
can do what George Cusack, Jr., did!" Cusack, Weigall
judged from the accompanying photo, was a little half-
witted anyway. If he could make $500,000 in four weeks
in Florida real estate, anybody could.

When, a couple of days later, Weigall stepped off a
train into the blazing August sunlight of a Miami after-
noon, he felt as though he had stepped into a tropical
bedlam. Amid the din of automobile horns, drills, ham-
mers, and winches, he later wrote, "Hatless, coatless
men rushed about the blazing streets, their arms full of
papers, perspiration pouring from their foreheads.
Every shop seemed to be combined with a real-estate

office; at every doorway crowds of young men were shouting and speech-making, thrusting forward papers and proclaiming to heaven the unsurpassed chances which they were offering to make a fortune. One had been prepared for real-estate madness; and here it was, *in excelsis*." Miami, Weigall was informed, was "one hell of a place . . . the finest city, sir, in the U.S.A., and I don't mean mebbe."

The mob scene that Weigall was swept into was without question one of the supreme spectacles of the palmy years of the twenties, a full dress rehearsal for the great bull market of 1929. The ebullience of Weigall's account merely reflects the excitement it inspired in almost every witness. The journalists and publicists who wrote of it nearly exhausted their stock of superlatives. The New York *Times* reported that more "pioneers de luxe" had settled in Florida within two years than in California in the ten years after the forty-niners. "All of America's gold rushes," Mark Sullivan wrote, looking back at the spectacle from the vantage point of the thirties, "all her oil booms, and all her free-land stampedes dwindled by comparison . . . with the torrent of migration pouring into Florida."

Amid that torrent of ambitious humanity, young Weigall soon realized that success was not automatic. He answered a newspaper advertisement and became a glorified salesman representing the "membership committee" of an exclusive but nonexistent "International Yacht Club," and eventually found his role turning out promotion copy for the Miami subdivision of Coral Gables. He was here at last in the vortex of the boom.

Coral Gables, unlike many of the fraudulent and

jerry-built promotions that imitated it, was the embodiment of an aesthetic vision. It had gestated for years in the mind of George E. Merrick, one of the towering geniuses of the Miami boom. He had come to Miami in the late nineties with his father, the Reverend Solomon Merrick, a New England Congregational minister who hoped the Florida climate would improve his wife's health. On a 160-acre tract south of town, the elder Merrick built a home he called Coral Gables after the local coral limestone and after Grey Gables, Grover Cleveland's house on Cape Cod. He established a business selling fruit and vegetables in the village of Miami, and young George, on his daily trips to town with produce, trusted directions to his horse and spent the time reading, composing poetry, and building castles in Spain, castles that would eventually become the city of Coral Gables.

The family orchards prospered enough to begin shipping carloads to the North, and George went away to college and, later, to law school. When his father died in 1911, he was forced to return home and manage the family estate. Merrick built up one of the most prosperous fruit and vegetable plantations in the area and in 1914 moved into the real-estate business, developing some of the earliest subdivisions around Miami. His ultimate dream, though, was of a new model city, "wherein nothing would be unlovely," an American Venice planned not only for comfort and convenience but for aesthetic quality. "For ten years," he later told a reporter, "I worked night and day to build up a nucleus for the Coral Gables which consistently grew in my dreams.

I never told anyone my plans, but as my profits in real estate grew, I bought adjoining land. The 160 acres the family originally owned increased to 300, then to 500 . . . and finally to 1,600."

Meanwhile, the situation slowly ripened for the realization of young Merrick's dream. For despite the impression it gave, the Florida boom did not spring to life full blown, like Aphrodite from the waves. It stemmed from a long line of promoters like Henry M. Flagler. The Florida historians A. J. and Kathryn Hanna have suggested that the Gold Coast from Hobe Sound, north of Palm Beach, to Miami could look back to Flagler "much as the human race recollects Noah." Before Flagler, Miami was but a lonely outpost on one of the last American frontiers. It had begun during the Seminole War of 1835–1842 with the establishment of Fort Dallas at the point where the Miami River empties into Biscayne Bay. Until the nineties the little settlements that grew around the fort were populated by fishermen, traders, small farmers, and a few refugees from northern winters.

Flagler, an early partner of John D. Rockefeller in Standard Oil, had first seen Florida on a vacation trip in 1878. He returned to St. Augustine for his honeymoon in 1883 and soon embarked upon a career of developing a string of resorts along Florida's eastern coast. Starting with two hotels at St. Augustine, the Ponce de Leon and the Alcazar, and with the improvement of railroad connections from Jacksonville, he pushed his Florida East Coast Railway on south to Ormond and Daytona, and eventually, in 1894, into Palm Beach. That year, Flagler added to his hotel chain by building the Royal Poinciana in Palm Beach, and, two years later, the Breakers. These hotels, supplemented by a railroad parking lot for private palace cars, were for decades among the favorite resorts of the rich and famous. When in April 1896, the railroad reached Miami, Flagler launched the city by constructing still another Flagler hotel, the Royal Palm; an electric light plant; and a water and sewage system. By 1900, Miami could claim a grand total of 1,681 persons.

On June 13, 1913, a few weeks after Flagler's death, a landmark was dedicated in Miami. It was the first bridge to Miami Beach, the narrow strip of land that separates Biscayne Bay from the Atlantic. The bridge was the brain child of another great Florida pioneer, John S. Collins, a successful New Jersey horticulturist who, in the eighties, had invested $5,000 in a scheme to grow coconut palms in the area. Disappointed in that venture, Collins came to Miami himself in 1896, acquired land on Miami Beach with an eye to its future resort possibilities, and, for the time being, began raising avocados, potatoes, and bananas.

But in order to assure the development of the area, Collins realized that there had to be a bridge from Miami to the beach. In 1912, with the backing of his three sons and his son-in-law, Thomas J. Pancoast, he began his bridge across Biscayne Bay. Halfway across, the contracting company failed, and with his Jordan nearly crossed, Collins' money ran out. The plight of the venture was brought to the attention of Carl Graham Fisher, an Indianian who had founded the Indianapolis Speedway and the Prestolite Company and who, by good luck, was just then vacationing in Miami. Fisher

met Collins, was impressed with his plan, and took
$50,000 worth of bonds in the bridge, enough to com-
plete it.

Fisher also inaugurated some of the more bizarre
phases of Florida promotion. He dredged up the bottom of Biscayne Bay in order to fill a mangrove swamp,
then dredged up more mud to make artificial islands in
the bay. He incorporated the town of Miami Beach in
1915, and after World War I opened a campaign of
hotel-building and high-pressure advertising unlike
anything seen before in the country. Among his gim-
micks were Carl and Rosie, two elephants who hauled
carloads of children around the island. One even served
as a caddy for President Harding. Finally, Fisher conceived the idea of the Miami Beach bathing beauty.
According to Will Rogers, he was the "midwife" of
Florida, who "rehearsed the mosquitos till they wouldn't
bite you until after you'd bought."

Thanks to the spadework of men like Flagler, Collins,
and Fisher, Miami on the eve of the boom was already a
playground for the rich. South Bay Shore Drive on Biscayne Bay, south of the city, had emerged as a million-
aire's row in 1916 with the completion of the palatial
Villa Vizcaya, home of the harvester magnate James
Deering. In 1923 William H. Luden, the coughdrop
king, arrived for the season at his home on the Drive,
and William K. Vanderbilt came in his $3,000,000 yacht,
Alva. Senator T. Coleman Du Pont of Delaware was
staying at Flagler's Royal Palm Hotel, and Harvey S.
Firestone came to visit and then to buy a great Georgian-
style showplace. Other visitors of note that year included
Labor Secretary James J. Davis, chain-store genius J. C.

Penney, auto mogul William C. Durant, and the 1920 Democratic presidential candidate, James M. Cox, who purchased control of a Miami newspaper and transformed it into the Miami *Daily News*. A new resident was sometime-politician, sometime-evangelist William Jennings Bryan, who taught a Bible class for tourists every Sunday morning in the Royal Palm Park. But, naturally, the climax of the 1923 season was the arrival at the Flamingo Hotel of President and Mrs. Warren Harding.

Thus all was in readiness for the boom when, in 1924, the combination of Coolidge prosperity and the proliferation of Henry Ford's tin lizzies gave Americans extra money to spend and made Florida an accessible place in which to spend it. A number of factors contributed to the Florida boom. First of all, there was money to be made in land speculation. The value of Florida real estate had been climbing since the turn of the century, and the state was particularly attractive to investors after 1924, when it outlawed both income and inheritance taxes.

But there was another more subtle and complex factor—a paradoxical revolt against the very urbanization and industrialization which were producing the new prosperity. The businessman made his money in the heart of the city, Frederick Lewis Allen suggested in *Only Yesterday*, but he wanted to spend it in exotic surroundings, in "a Venice equipped with bathtubs and electric ice-boxes, a Seville provided with three eighteen-hole golf courses." Florida promoters lost no opportunity to make it abundantly clear that Florida was *the* exotic place. "Florida is bathed in passionate caresses of the southern sun," one advertisement read. "It is laved

by the limpid waves of the embracing seas, wooed by
the glorious Gulf Stream, whose waters, warmed by
the tropical sun, speed northeast to temper the climate
of Europe. Florida is an emerald kingdom by southern
seas, fanned by zephyrs laden with ozone from stately
pines, watered by Lethe's copious libation, decked with
palm and pine, flower and fern, clothed in perpetual
verdure and lapt in the gorgeous folds of the semi-
tropical zone." How could a small-town banker looking
out his window at the frozen wastes of North Dakota
resist *that*?

Every winter after the Armistice more and more
"snowbirds" appeared. They were very different from
the Vanderbilts and Du Ponts who had frequented Flagler's elegant hostelries. The arrivals of the twenties were
a part of what might be termed a "subdivision civilization," one which allowed the middle class to enjoy a
comparatively inexpensive season in the sun and, if they
were lucky, to turn a pretty penny in land speculation
besides.

The prototype of the Florida subdivision was Coral
Gables. By 1921, George Merrick had 1,600 acres just
southwest of Miami, $500,000, and a sound experience
in real-estate development. Now, with a highly organized
sales force and a stable of architects, he took the first
tentative steps toward making his dream city a reality,
cautiously building a road or two, putting in lighting
and water connections. The first sales of lots were made
in November, 1921. Within two years the sudden inflation of land values was under way, and Coral Gables
was one of the first areas to be caught up in the rapid
expansion. Almost overnight Merrick found himself

dealing in millions. He expanded his holdings to 10,000 acres, formed the Coral Gables Corporation under his sole control, and amid the speculative frenzy saw his dream begin to materialize.

Throughout the boom Merrick remained an enigma to the hosts of extroverts that swarmed into Miami. A large, squarely built, pensive man in his late thirties, he avoided personal publicity and consistently refused to attend public functions. Even his dress—ill-fitting tweed trousers, Norfolk jacket, and old brogues—seemed strangely un-Miami. T. H. Weigall still regarded him worshipfully years later as "a very great man," "passionately in love with Florida," not for the sake of its exploitation but as "the last outpost of the United States, a fresh and unspoiled territory which it would be criminal to let develop along haphazard, ugly, or unscientific lines."

As the boom advanced, development of Coral Gables accelerated: the area was landscaped; lakes and waterways connected to Biscayne Bay were blasted out; and winding avenues and plazas were built through the pine woods. The quarry from which the coral rock had been dug for construction was converted into the colorful Venetian Pool. Carefully planned residential and business sections began to emerge, as well as the University of Miami, which was expected to rival the great academic centers of the East. There were golf courses, a country club, and a twenty-six-story hotel, the Miami-Biltmore. Everything was to be in a blend of Spanish-Italian architecture that Merrick called "Mediterranean."

As Weigall described Coral Gables later, "Its main boulevards were all 100 feet wide, and at their intersections there were fountains surrounded by tropical trees and wide plazas paved with coral rock. Everywhere there was brilliantly-colored foliage and running water. Its houses stood well back in their gardens, and even the offices, with their brightly-colored sun-blinds, gave an impression of being almost countrified. Everywhere there were dazzling colors—white walls, striped awnings, red roofs, brilliant greenery, and the intense blue of the Florida sky." By the spring of 1925 it included five hundred homes.

Northward from Coral Gables the boom spirit spread up the coast and across the Florida peninsula into a hundred subdivisions of a hundred towns, each elaborating its own variations on Merrick's theme of a perfect city. There was Hollywood, the "Golden Gate of the South"; Fort Lauderdale, the "Tropical Wonderland"; Orlando, the "City Beautiful"; Winter Park, the "City of Homes"; Haines City, the "Gateway to the Scenic Highlands"; Sebring, the "Orange Blossom City"; Fort Myers, the "City of Palms"; and St. Petersburg, the "Sunshine City," where the *Independent* gave away its edition on any day the sun failed to shine.

Even staid old Palm Beach, at first inclined to look down its aristocratic nose upon the scrambling *nouveaux riches*, was caught up in the hurricane of expansion. Palm Beach was to be wooed and won into the heart of the boom by one of the great charlatan-geniuses of the twenties, Addison Mizner—painter, woodcarver, miner, interior decorator, prize fighter, writer, architect. Born in California in 1872, Mizner had gone to Guatemala with his father in his teens, and there had fallen in love with Spanish art and architecture. This love had later grown during a brief stay at the University of Salamanca in Spain. Over the years he had pursued his offbeat career as an exotic and romantic dilettante on four continents.

Mizner's first brush with fame had been as co-author of *The Cynic's Calendar*: "Where there's a will, there's a lawsuit"; "Many are called but few get up"; "The wages of gin is breath"; "Be held truthful that your lies may count." He was working in New York as a society architect and designer of Japanese landscapes when ill health carried him to Palm Beach in 1918.

There he fell in with a kindred spirit, Paris Singer, whose inheritance from his father's sewing machines gave him the time and the money to pursue both the arts and Isadora Duncan. Soon the combination of the Florida sun and Singer's generosity had helped Mizner recover to the point that he was busily designing a hospital financed by Singer—for convalescent World War I soldiers. But the war was completed before the hospital was, and it was transformed into the Everglades Club, displacing Flagler's Breakers as the *ne plus ultra* of Palm Beach. The Everglades was the first of many architectural triumphs that established Mizner as the supreme master of the Florida Spanish motif. It led to a commission for him to build a villa for banker Edward T. Stotesbury, the first of dozens of rich patrons—including G. Rodman Wanamaker II, Drexel Biddle, Jr., and a pride of Vanderbilts—who were eager to pay for the privilege of being insulted by a great architect and of living in the gigantic pleasure domes he created for them.

The architecture of these latter-day Xanadus has been summarized by Alva Johnston in his book, *The*

Legendary Mizners, as the Bastard-Spanish-Moorish-Romanesque-Gothic-Renaissance-Bull-Market-Damn-the-Expense Style. Their central theme was inevitably Spanish, but Mizner, a versatile antiquarian, sometimes threw ten centuries into one structure. "Most modern architects," he said, "have spent their lives in carrying out a period to the last letter and producing a characterless copybook effect. My ambition has been to take the reverse stand—to make a building look traditional and as though it had fought its way from a small unimportant structure to a great rambling house that took centuries of different needs and ups and downs of wealth to accomplish. I sometimes start a house with a Romanesque corner, pretend that it has fallen into disrepair and been added to in the Gothic spirit, when suddenly the great wealth of the New World has poured in and the owner has added a very rich Renaissance addition."

To get the all-important appearance of antiquity Mizner inflicted the wildest vandalism on his masterpieces. He deliberately smudged up new rooms with burning pots of tarpaper, took penknife and sledgehammer to woodwork and statuary, used ice picks and air rifles on furniture, hired inexperienced help to lay roof tiles awry, and once had men in hobnailed boots walk up and down a stairway before the cement set to get the effect of centuries of wear. One of his original contributions to architecture was the discovery that worm-eaten cypress gave the desired effect of age; thus pecky cypress, formerly considered almost worthless, suddenly became the mahogany of Palm Beach.

The one talent Mizner lacked was that of making conventional plans and specifications. Everything was done off-the-cuff. Plans for one house were drawn in the sand on the beach, a window in another was copied from a photograph of a house on Minorca. When one client asked for a blueprint, Mizner replied in amazement, "Why, the house isn't built yet." Occasionally, this resulted in oversights, such as the failure to include a staircase in one mansion; a staircase was eventually added— but outside, so that it would not spoil the perfection of the interior.

His landscaping experience gave him a distinct feelling for the setting of a house. To an admirer, the journalist Ida Tarbell, he seemed "to have a veritable passion for utilizing all the natural beauties of the place," an ability "to make a typical Florida thing." Vistas of the ocean, the blue skies, the tall palms, all figured in his craft. Large windows and cross drafts let the balmy air into his rooms. He noticed that the prevailing winds were from the southwest, so his kitchens were invariably in the northeast corner of the house. As an artist he understood the dramatic effects of color—he preferred pastels. He looted Spain and Central America of tile roofs and furnishings and set up his own Mizner Industries, Inc., to make the latest thing in "antiques," wrought iron, artificial stone, stained glass, terra cotta, tiles, urns, pots, and fountains.

Not far from the Everglades Club were the Via Mizner, the Via Parigi, and the Worth Avenue Arcade, where Mizner created Old World alleys of little shops and sidewalk cafés with gay pink, blue, and cream-colored fronts. Up and down Palm Beach his talent ran riot, spawning a city of palaces with great watch towers and thick walls, cloistered arcades, high galleries, vaulted ceilings, and tiled pools. These edifices have been called by some the work of a quack, by others, including Frank Lloyd Wright, that of a genius.

Addison Mizner soon had a million dollars, he claimed, salted away in government bonds, but it was inevitable that he would be drawn into the subdivision madness that swept up from Miami. He was joined in that adventure by his scape-grace brother, Wilson, a latter-day Sir John Falstaff who had come down from New York in 1921 to manage Mizner Industries. He was a master of the pulverizing phrase and was credited by some with the quip, "Never give a sucker an even break."

As the boom roared into fantastic excesses, Wilson found himself more and more at home in the Florida wonderland. The Mizners got a late start, but they made up for it by projecting the most ostentatious subdivision of all at Boca Raton (Rat's Mouth), a little stop on the Florida East Coast Railway south of Palm Beach. The plans featured El Camino Real, a highway 219 feet wide and only about twelve times as long, with twenty traffic lanes and a "Venetian canal" with powered gondolas running down its center. There was to be a hotel, an airport, a polo field, two golf courses, a yacht basin, and a church that was to be a memorial to Mama Mizner and a source of satisfaction to the Mizners' other brother, an Episcopal priest—the white sheep, as it were, of the family. Unfortunately, little of it got off Addison's mental drawing boards. "Beaucoup Rotten," the rival realtors labeled it, and so it turned out to be, for it got under way as the boom roared to a collapse. The only structure completed was the hotel, the Cloister, one of Addison's masterpieces.

At mid-decade the boom spirit soared to its peak. The Gold Coast, of which Miami was the heart, was geared to a winter-resort economy; from April to November it subsided into lassitude. But in 1925 the season never ended. The swarms of "tin can" tourists continued to arrive in their flivvers throughout that summer. Kenneth L. Roberts, covering the scene for the *Saturday Evening Post*, estimated that 4,000 people a day entered the state by automobile, supplemented by another 3,000 on trains and 200 on ships, making perhaps more than 2,500,000 in the boom year.

The new arrivals included a liberal sprinkling of real and pseudo celebrities. Indeed, the number of celebrities a town or subdivision had was considered a good barometer of its prestige. Thus Miami Beach boasted that it was the resort of "America's wealthiest sportsmen, devotees of yachting and other expensive sports." The subdivision of Floranda had the Earl and Countess Lauderdale, Lord Thirlestane, and the former king of Greece; Gene Tunney regularly appeared at another subdivision; Bobby Jones was at Davis Islands in Tampa Bay: Helen Morgan and Elsie Janis could be seen at Hollywood-by-the-Sea. And Florida's famous visitors did not have to go around thirsty in the sun just because of the Eighteenth Amendment. Liquor was as readily available as it was in Al Capone's Chicago. The primary source for this cheer was the Bahamas. In 1922 a friend just back from Nassau reported to a horrified William Jennings Bryan, "The Bahamians are very proud of the fact that Prohibition in the United States has made their country independent. They boast of the fact that theirs is the only government known to be out of debt, with millions in the Treasury and a monthly income of more than $500,000 in revenue from the sales of whiskey alone."

Amidst this combination of boom times, dazzling celebrities, and free-flowing booze, the most ludicrous scenes became commonplace. At the Miami Western Union office those unable to reach the desk wrapped their messages in rocks and tossed them over the heads of the crowd. Every evening on the streets of Miami, charabancs of "realtors" passed slowly through the crowds shouting out their bargains to the accompaniment of trombones and saxophones. One of the most conspicuous features in promotion was the boom orator. There were all kinds among these spellbinders: sideshow barkers, auctioneers, and free-lance orators willing to talk on any subject for a minimum of ten dollars an hour. Bible-Belt gospel shouters, many of them carried away with a semireligious enthusiasm for Florida, earned premium wages. "It was a common sight," Weigall reported, "at any wayside barbecue on the Dixie Highway, to see some purple-faced orator mounted on the back seat of his car under the blazing sun bellowing of the land of hope to an awestruck audience standing round him in the white dust."

It was scarcely an exaggeration to say that everybody in Miami was "in real estate" in one way or another. The city was finally forced to pass an ordinance against making sales in the street or on the sidewalks. Since all ordinary office and salesroom space was taken up, the realtors had to operate from partitioned sections of hotel lobbies and warehouses, in cleared basements, enclosed porches, and boxed-in spaces between buildings.

In the better-organized operations, lots were sold from blueprints or models. D. P. Davis promoted development at St. Augustine with a forty-foot mock-up that featured tiny powered boats running around a minuscule island. Actually to see the lots was not possible, since they were offered "predevelopment," before the streets had been laid, the yacht basin opened, or even the mud dredged up to raise the land above water level. Underwater lots were among the standard frauds, but customers stood in line—some of them reportedly for forty hours—to buy lots on Davis Islands in Tampa Bay and Venetian Islands in Biscayne Bay while they were still under water. (Surprisingly, these particular speculations returned a tidy profit to the investors when the operations proved successful.)

To attend the opening of a subdivision sale, one frequently needed a reservation. Many a customer, having made a down payment of 10 percent, would step up when his turn came, select a lot from the blueprint, see it stamped "Sold," accept his receipt, and then rush out in search of a buyer. In the speculative fairyland of fast turnover and quick fortunes, the careless plunger was more likely to profit than the prudent investor. No matter how outrageous the price, there always seemed to be somebody else to whom one could "pass the baby" for more money.

Even well-planned Coral Gables became more and more involved in the boom-time hoopla. Merrick soon had three thousand salesmen hawking building lots and a fleet of seventy-six buses "to take you to Coral Gables at any time you desire"—as a guest of the corporation. The Coral Gables fleet made regular runs to and from the larger southern cities and occasional runs to and from New York, Chicago, and even San Francisco. And to guarantee that prospective buyers would be in a re-

ceptive mood once they reached his heaven on the Atlantic, Merrick had band leaders Paul Whiteman and
Jan Garber making sweet music at the Venetian Pool,
with "When the Moon Shines on Coral Gables" one of
their most popular numbers. In addition, from a platform in the pool itself, the champion of silver, William
Jennings Bryan, earned a little gold by orating on the
miracle of Miami; it was, Bryan declared, "the only city
in the world where you can tell a lie at breakfast that
will come true by evening." For trumpeting this cheer-
ing news, Bryan received an annual salary of more than
fifty thousand dollars. And just in case Bryan didn't do
the trick, he was sometimes followed by the original
"shimmy girl," Gilda Gray, who shook her chemise with
such gusto that it took the viewers' minds off the prices
quoted for lots by salesmen circulating through the
audience.

But the Mizners' Boca Raton was not about to play
second string to Merrick's Coral Gables or any other
subdivision in the Florida promotion game. Wilson Mizner imported an old friend, the publicist Harry T.
Reichenbach, to make Boca Raton into what Wilson
called a "platinum sucker trap." The bait—overpower-
ing snob appeal. It was announced that only the "best"
people could get into the place, which meant, quite
simply, only those with lots of ready cash. (Palm Beach,
Wilson said, would be converted into servants' quarters
for Boca Raton.) In Reichenbach's unmeasured terms,
it was the habitat of "the world of international wealth
that dominates finance and industry . . . that sets fashion
. . . the world of large affairs, smart society and leisured
ease." The Mizners collected, among other celebrities,
two Du Ponts, one Vanderbilt, Elizabeth Arden, Irving

Berlin, Herbert Bayard Swope, James M. Cox, George Whitney, and Marie Dressler, "the Duchess of Boca Raton." At one point sales of lots, on paper, averaged two million dollars a week.

The legends of money to be made in Florida real estate began to rival those of the California Gold Rush. Kenneth Roberts told of a strip of land in Palm Beach that was sold in 1915 for $84,000, in 1922 for $240,000, in 1923 for $800,000, in 1924 for $1,500,000; in 1925 it was estimated to be worth nearly $5,000,000. Weigall knew a New York bank clerk who went to Florida with a thousand dollars and returned three weeks later with $375,000, which he had the good sense to invest in gilt-edged securities. A New York cab driver who took a passenger, who could not get train accommodations, all the way to Miami, stayed, and made a fortune speculating with the money he earned driving his cab. Land on West Flagler Street in Miami, which had been worth $30 an acre in 1910, was bringing $75,000 an acre by 1925.

But it was the "binder boys" who perfected into a fine art a method of making profits on little or no investment. The principle was to pay a nominal "binder" fee on the promise of a down payment to be made perhaps a month later and additional payments "as of one, two, and three years." The profit then would be reaped by the simple process of trading binders which might pass through a dozen or more hands before the initial down payment was made. The practice was finally broken up by Miami realtors who caught a group of smart operators from New York on binders and quickly produced abstracts with an agreement that cash payment was due immediately.

Even the clearest vision seemed to become dazzled by all this glitter. Both Weigall and Reichenbach actually began to believe that there was genuine twenty-four karat gold to be had in speculation, and plunged in with their own savings. Roger Babson, who was to make his reputation by warning of the 1929 stock market crash, predicted an endless rosy future in Florida real estate.

It was all too good to last. Here and there skeptics began to raise their voices. Walter J. Greenbaum, a Chicago investment banker, warned against "wildcat land speculation" in Florida, and the Massachusetts Savings Bank League cautioned depositors against withdrawing money to invest there. Walter C. Hill of the Atlanta Retail Credit Company predicted that it would all end in the winter of 1925/1926. The alarm seemed especially severe in Ohio. State Commerce Director Cyrus Locher went to Florida to investigate. "When the boom has subsided, there will be headaches all over America," he reported. "The rise in Florida will continue as long as northern money is sent to Florida, and the end will be that of every boom, where few prosper and many hold the bag at the end." Ohio passed "blue sky" laws in 1925 forbidding certain firms to sell Florida property.

These doubts suddenly began to take their toll of confidence. It was calculated that within ten miles of Miami there were enough building lots on the market to provide sites for houses for two million people. The first hard sign that the boom was going sour came when a lot on Miami Beach, which had been sold for $50,000, brought only $25,000. Other clouds, too, began to appear in the sunny Florida skies. In the summer of 1925, a fire started by an electric hair curler burned down both the Breakers and the Palm Beach Hotel. Then, Flagler's East Coast Line and the Seaboard found that their tracks had taken so much punishment from increased boom traffic that urgent repairs were necessary at once. To make this possible, an embargo was declared in August, 1925, on all carload lots except fuel, petroleum, livestock, and perishable material. In September, a "less than carload lot" embargo went into effect.

The embargo had disastrous effects on the boom, leaving thousands of desperate builders with unfinished construction on their hands. (One frantic contractor smuggled in a carload of bricks buried in ice and labeled "lettuce.") The only alternative was to bring in material by water, and scores of abandoned hulks were resurrected for the purpose. But in January, 1926, an old Danish training ship, the *Prinz Valdemar*, which was being renovated to serve as a floating cabaret in the Miami harbor, capsized in the middle of the channel, completely halting all inbound and outbound shipping for several weeks.

As though these problems were not enough, other developments cast further gloom. For one thing, federal income-tax troubles began to dog the speculators. The rumors of a tax reduction in 1926, and the report that a number of special revenue agents had been sent into Florida, led many speculators to hold up sales in order to postpone profits until January, 1926. In December, 1925, the Internal Revenue Service announced that all notes on real-estate transactions would be considered as cash received and that full tax payment was due on them. The National Better Business Bureaus commenced an investigation of frauds in Florida real estate, and a stock market break in February and March of 1926 forced back to New York many businessmen who had gone to Florida to plunge.

Through Christmas week, 1925, Miami was able to disguise its nagging doubts behind a cheerful holiday mask. On Christmas Eve the New York *Times* reported that rents were coming down, but the planned festivities went on. In a joint statement the mayors of Miami, Miami Beach, Hialeah, and Coral Gables proclaimed the last day of 1925 and the first two days of 1926 "The Fiesta of the American Tropics," a season "when Love, Good Fellowship, Merrymaking, and Wholesome Sport shall prevail throughout Our Domains." They declared that "through our Streets and Avenues shall wind a glorious Pageantry of Sublime Beauty Depicting in Floral Loveliness the Blessing Bestowed upon us by Friendly Sun, Gracious Rain, and Soothing Tropic Wind." But the market would no longer respond to this kind of ballyhoo. The new season saw real-estate prices breaking sharply as optimists whistled in the dark about "stabilization," "leveling-off," and "salutary readjustment." On February 14, 1926, the New York *Times* reported a decided lull. By July, Stella Crossley wrote bluntly in the *Nation*: "The Florida boom has collapsed. The world's greatest poker game, played with building lots instead of chips, is over. And the players are now cashing in or paying up." The roads north, she said, were black with "a strangely quiet exodus."

The coup de grâce to the boom was administered by a formidable tropical hurricane, with winds in excess of 128 miles an hour, which roared over the Gold Coast and the Everglades on September 18, 1926. The storm killed 115 people in the Miami area and another 300 in the village of Moore Haven when it was flooded by the waters of Lake Okeechobee. Miami Beach was entirely inundated, and at one point during the storm the ocean extended deep into Miami itself. Four thousand homes were destroyed and nine thousand more damaged in the area from Fort Lauderdale to Miami, with property losses in the Greater Miami area alone put at $76,000,000.

Yet the wreckage left by the hurricane was as nothing compared to the wreckage left by the collapse of the boom. On Singer's Island, just north of Palm Beach, an unfinished hotel begun by Paris Singer became a luxurious resort for sea birds. In Miami, a hotel near the airport was transformed into a haven, not for snowbirds but for chickens. With property holders defaulting to creditors and to the tax collector, the only land-office business in Florida was being done in the courts.

The Mizners' Boca Raton was never finished, and the brothers, when they died in 1933, were both financially ruined. But Addison left behind more than a score of houses that are among the supreme artistic artifacts of the twenties. George Merrick's Coral Gables, which had never relaxed its rigid zoning or its architectural standards, remained one of the most beautiful towns in America. And though Merrick himself lost heavily when the bubble burst, he made something of a comeback. In 1934 he reentered the real-estate business and soon had branch offices throughout Greater Miami. When he died in 1942 he was Miami's postmaster.

Not all of the new arrivals of the twenties departed when the bubble burst. Miami's population had grown from 5,471 in 1910 to 29,571 in 1920; it had risen to

110,637 by 1930. In the twenties the metropolitan area led all others in the nation in its rate of growth, and the twin cities of Tampa and St. Petersburg ranked sixth. And in the thirties, Florida as a whole continued to grow at a more rapid rate than any other state in the Union. But, when compared to the boom time of the twenties and the boom time which was to come in the fifties, the peninsula was as in a great sleep.

In 1928, Henry S. Villard described a trip to Miami for the *Nation*: "Dead subdivisions line the highway, their pompous names half-obliterated on crumbling stucco gates. Lonely, white-way lights stand guard over miles of cement sidewalks, where grass and palmetto take the place of homes that were to be. . . . Whole sections of outlying subdivisions are composed of un-occupied houses, through which one speeds on broad thoroughfares as if traversing a city in the grip of death."

10

The "Colonial Economy" and the Growth Psychology: The South in the Thirties

SOME TIME AGO AN ADVERTISEMENT APPEARED IN THE pages of the New York *Times*.

> Pinpoint your growth opportunities in SCIENTIFIC TEN-
> NESSEE [it said]. If you're a science-oriented industry, you'll
> be right at home in Scientific Tennessee! The state is rich
> in technology with 24 research centers, 47 colleges and
> universities, Arnold Engineering Development Center,
> Oak Ridge National Laboratory, University of Tennessee
> Space Institute and many scientific companies. Shouldn't
> you see about Tennessee . . . now?

That advertisement appeared almost exactly forty years
(lacking three weeks) after the sovereign state of Tennessee had outlawed the teaching of science! Its contrast
to the spirit of the antievolution law is but one token of
the striking changes that have taken place in the South
during the last generation. And it is, one may reasonably
expect, a token of the future in this age of technology
and research.

The issues of the thirties seem in many ways strangely
archaic today. The nation entered that decade in the

grip of the worst depression in its history, and the economic problems of the period afforded a peculiar focus for a growing regional consciousness in the South. It was a time not only of depression but of the New Deal and rising sectional feeling in politics; a time of literary renaissance, the Vanderbilt Agrarians, and the Chapel Hill Regionalists; a decade at the end of which John Temple Graves said the South was "more aware of itself as a region than it had been since 1861."

A good part of that awareness turned on the economic plight of the South, and nearly every New Deal effort to meet the national crisis contributed to the awareness by inadvertently raising sectional issues. The recovery program was one example among many. The purposes of the National Recovery Administration (NRA), briefly stated, were two-fold: (1) to stabilize business through codes of "fair" competitive practice, and (2) to increase purchasing power by assuring employment and raising wages. Southern businessmen at first shared the national enthusiasm for the effort. Already many of them had joined in voluntary efforts to restrain overproduction. Stabilization through trade associations, such as the Cotton Textile Institute, promised manifest advantages of more predictable costs and markets, as well as more stable employment and wages. "The law of life is cooperation, and not selfish cut-throat competition," said one of the leading trade journals.

Yet the doctrine of stabilization, at least in the depression years, was largely the restrictive doctrine of a mature economy that had reached substantially all its frontiers of expansion. Both in theory and practice it ran headlong into conflict with the doctrine of industrial growth that was written in the prophets of a New South.

Stabilization offered certain assurances to the businessman, but it threatened to nullify the region's competitive advantages. The point had been expressed succinctly by a South Carolina manufacturer, in objection to an earlier voluntary movement for restraint. Night operations in the South hurt New England, he noted, "and for this I am not sorry. If we should discourage night operations in South Carolina, overproduction would immediately stop, but as a consequence, New England would start up all of her idle spindles." And that was substantially the result of the NRA textile code, which limited operations to eighty hours a week. The rule curtailed production in the South but permitted New England mills to increase their activity.

New labor standards under the NRA created a parallel dilemma. They, too, met a favorable reception at first, but inevitably they collided with the low-wage philosophy that was the corollary—almost the central theme—of the southern growth psychology. A major impulse to industrialization was the urge to lift regional standards of material well-being. But any action to raise southern wages, the reasoning went, would threaten the region's supreme competitive advantage (its cheap labor), would hamper industrial development, and therefore prolong the very poverty it was supposed to relieve. The argument, frequently embellished with claims of lower living costs in the South, was repeatedly advanced against efforts to improve labor conditions: the NRA, relief, unionism, legislation on wages and hours.

As recovery gradually seeped back, eroding the cement of fear, the NRA inspired a growing irritation and disillusionment. Charges mounted that the larger corporations dominated code authorities, that allocations froze the existing industrial structure, that price-fixing denied small manufacturers opportunities for competition. In the South the complaints assumed a sectional tone. "You know," George Fort Milton of Chattanooga wrote the secretary of commerce in 1934, "that a great many of our Southern industrialists suspect . . . that much of the glee about NRA is because it is going to permit obsolete units of the north and east to better themselves at the expense of the South." No region, the *Texas Business Review* remarked, would stand "to gain more than the Gulf Southwest in any sound policy which has for its aim the expansion of industry based upon sound competition. Conversely no region would stand to suffer greater loss if a policy of permanent restriction were to be adopted."

But the crux of the issue was wages. "Now, we are referred to in other parts of the country as the low-wage section," a former president of the National Association of Manufacturers (NAM), John E. Edgerton of Tennessee, told the Southern Pine Association. "As a matter of fact the N.R.A. was devised, to a very large extent, to reform the South. . . . General Johnson practically told me that when he said, 'We don't propose to allow the Negro labor of the South to debase the living standards of the rest of the country.'" Actually, however, the recovery act permitted wage differentials favorable to southern industry. Nevertheless, code wages generally lifted southern rates substantially, by 50 to 100 percent, according to the *Manufacturers Record*.

The increases quickly generated an organized opposition. In 1933 Edgerton undertook to organize the

Southern States Industrial Council "to protect the South against discrimination"—that is, against higher wages. The council was "a child of the N.R.A.," Edgerton told a Senate committee. "It sprang into . . . spontaneous existence, immediately after the codes began to become operative." The code wages, a sympathetic *Manufacturers Record* declared, would "hamper present manufacturing activity, industrial development, and the fullest utilization of Southern resources in the future." Businessmen whose comment the magazine sought agreed. "I do not believe that any section has responded more enthusiastically to the requirements of the Industrial Recovery Act than has the South," an Augusta manufacturer wrote, "nor paid more heavily for the response." The sole dissent came from a maverick lumberman in Memphis who thought the South needed more purchasing power and more contented, well-paid labor.

When the NRA died in 1935, few paused to mourn, but it left a heritage of sectional feeling that would be nourished further by the rise of the union movement and the drive for legislation on wages and hours. But by mid-decade the economic weather had changed. The New South spirit of Henry Grady was a hardy perennial that lay dormant only for a brief winter of depression; before the end of the thirties it was in as full bloom as ever. "Depression is forgotten in the South," *Business Week* reported at the end of 1936. "The industrial expansion is on again, full swing, and things are booming." During that year a dynamic growth began in two fields. New chemical plant construction across the South absorbed more than 33 million dollars and the building of a new Union Bag and Paper Company at Savannah provoked a scramble among papermakers to establish priority at other likely ports and subjugate the tributary woodlands. The South's share of national paper production bounded up from 12.4 percent in 1935 to 17.2 percent in 1937. The peculiar significance of paper was that it brought industry to the piney woods and offered an answer to the old problem of cutover lands.

By the end of 1938 an anonymous writer in *Fortune*. envisioned a future that suggested "serious modifications" in pessimistic theories of economic maturity. Southern potentialities were "a denial of saturation," he wrote. Kraft paper and chemicals were new industries, adding much more to the economy than they took away from older enterprises. It was likely, therefore, he suggested, "that the further development of the South . . . may provide the evidence needed to disprove the theories of those who hold that industrial expansion has about reached its limit."

Meanwhile, the old spirit of industrial promotion revived. In 1936 Mississippi inaugurated a statewide program of factory subsidies under its "balance agriculture with industry" scheme, the vanguard of new or enlarged state industrial promotions that mushroomed over the next few years. Notwithstanding serious doubts that such programs had more than peripheral effect upon plant location or attracted anything but low-wage industries, they probably stood on a stronger foundation of public support than ever before. Events of the depression years had underscored the susceptibility of a raw-material economy to violent fluctuations and the value even of sweatshops in raising southern incomes.

But industry-hunting posed still another dilemma. The quest for capital and branch plants led inevitably

to the metropolitan North, with the unavoidable consequences of outside control and the drain of profits out
of the region. But the importation of capital had been
by and large the story of industrial development in the
region since the Civil War, and qualms about alien control or exploitation seldom deterred the local boosters,
eager to develop their natural resources of cheap labor.
They made little effort to spur indigenous development—in part, one observer thought, because of a persistent agricultural tradition and a "regional inferiority
complex where industry is concerned." The capital deficiency of the South was aggravated by "the spectacle
of . . . Southerners turning down industrial investments
of a few thousand dollars that would return them many
hundred per cent" for investments in national corporations and in land "not . . . producing nearly enough to
justify its valuation." The South manifestly could not—
and would not—lift itself by its own bootstraps.

The economic trials of the thirties afforded a backdrop for the emergence of regional analysis. In 1936
Howard W. Odum published his monumental *Southern
Regions*, the climax to more than a decade of development in regional sociology. The scope of the study was
broad, but its focus was regional development and its
implications to a great extent economic. The indices of
southern deficiency that Odum so ponderously cataloged pointed ultimately to a source in poverty and that,
in turn, to a source in the one-crop agriculture and one-
crop industry of the region. The South, Odum wrote at
one point, had been "essentially colonial in its economy,"
suffering "the general status of an agricultural country
engaged in trade with industrial countries."

The concept of the "colonial economy," thus expressed by Odum in rudimentary form, summarized an earlier treatment by his younger colleague, Rupert Vance, whose *Human Geography of the South* apparently first gave currency to the term. Viewing the South in historical perspective, Vance in one chapter of his *Human Geography* had traced the region's evolution through successive conquests of new frontiers, the development of an extractive economy that progressively exploited natural resources and cheap labor without any appreciable accumulation of capital, that looked to the outside for financing and exported much of the return. In the beginning the definition of *colonial economy* was expressed basically in terms of a distinction between primary and secondary production. The South produced chiefly raw materials and industrial roughage for the market-oriented industries of the North, and as a primary producer, remained in a dependent and tributary status, performing those functions that carry the least rewards in a modern economy.

But in its further development the colonial concept grew into the idea of a region deliberately and systematically plundered by outside forces. Charles A. Beard had already established a foundation for this idea with his economic interpretation of sectional struggle in the nineteenth century. Walter Prescott Webb, a historian at the University of Texas, elaborated the new concept in his *Divided We Stand: The Crisis of a Frontierless Democracy*. In Webb, the scholar merged with the polemicist who identified with dramatic skill the villains of the piece. They were the great corporations with their patent controls, their restrictive licensing arrangements, their discriminatory pricing systems, their insurance company investments in northern industry, their deliberate measures to subjugate the South and West under "economic imperial control by the North." The Republican party was their chief ally, with its policies of tariffs, subsidies, patents, and regionalized freight rates, even Civil War pensions which had provided purchasing power for northern business and relieved the treasury's embarrassment of riches from tariff revenues.

Variations on the theme reverberated in periodicals and public discussion for more than a decade. The South's lack of specialty enterprises, economist C. T. Murchison noted, "leaves the South with the worst form of economic disadvantage, that of having to exchange a few bulky staple products for the myriads of highly manufactured specialty goods which she must consume." The South's adverse balance of trade, a southern editor told David Cushman Coyle in 1937, was probably a billion dollars annually. The debit was balanced by selling property to outside investors, by borrowing, going bankrupt, or by exhausting lands and timber for immediate cash. "The South actually works for the North," Maury Maverick declared; "mortgage, insurance, industrial, and finance corporations pump the money northward like African ivory out of the Congo." "We are confronted with a paradox more amazing and ironical than any ever conjured by the imagination of Gilbert and Sullivan," B. B. Kendrick told the Southern Historical Association in 1941. "The people of the South, who all their lives had suffered deprivation, want, and humiliation from an outside finance imperialism, followed with hardly a murmur of protest leaders who, if indirectly, were nonetheless in effect agents and attorneys of the imperialists." The thesis has had a continuing influence on historians. C. Vann Woodward included a chapter entitled "The Colonial Economy" in his *Origins of the New South, 1877–1913*. "As a means of discouraging the rise of competing manufacturers, building up a monopoly of the carrying trade, promoting an ample supply of cheap raw materials, and eliminating foreign competition in colonial markets," Woodward wrote, "the combination of regionalized freight rates, basing-point system, Pittsburgh Plus, Birmingham Differential, patent control, and Federal tariff schedules was rather more effective than the combination of Navigation Acts, Wool Act, Iron Act, and Hat Act."

During the thirties a kind of climax to the literature of the colonial economy came in the *Report on Economic Conditions of the South* sponsored by the National Emergency Council in 1938. The report was proposed to the president by Clark Foreman of Atlanta, then an official of the Public Works Administration and formerly advisor to Harold Ickes on Negro affairs. And Foreman largely directed its preparation by a group of southerners in federal service. Many hands contributed to the final result, but it was essentially a synopsis of existing analyses by Vance, Odum, Webb and others. "The paradox of the South," the report declared, "is that while it is blessed by Nature with immense wealth, its people as a whole are the poorest in the country. Lacking industries of its own, the South has been forced to trade the richness of its soil, its minerals and forests, and the labor of its people for goods manufactured elsewhere." The report proceeded in sixty-four pages and fourteen sections to outline problems of soil and water resources, population, income, education, health, housing, labor, tenancy, credit, exploitation of natural resources, industry, and purchasing power. It attacked, particularly, damage to the regional economy by tariffs, regional freight rates, monopoly, and absentee ownership.

Publication of the report placed the Roosevelt administration squarely behind the sectional rebellion against colonial bondage and strongly implied administration support for a coordinated effort of regional development. Moreover, the president deliberately linked it to his efforts for a political realignment in 1938. In August, when he launched the ill-fated primary campaign against Senator Walter F. George, he announced the publication of the report, and repeated a part of his earlier remarks to the report's sponsoring committee.

"It is my conviction," the president had said in July, "that the South presents right now, in 1938, the Nation's No. 1 economic problem." The report went forth, coupled with that catch-phrase, so well tailored to the headlines. It was almost as if the president had pushed the button that activated the conditioned reflex of the sensitive South, and many of the responses assumed the phrase to be another purblind stereotype of the benighted South. The region had accomplished much in the past seventy-five years, Senator Josiah W. Bailey of North Carolina declared indignantly, because of "our forefathers who rebuilt the South after the Civil War." What the South needed most, Senator John E. Miller of Arkansas asserted, was to be left alone. In the furor of that political summer the import of the president's position was lost and his effort to harness the power of sectional feeling to the New Deal cause failed completely.

Insofar as the concept of the colonial economy became a political force it ran in a rather narrow channel. As so often happens with complex issues it came to a focus on one specific grievance, discriminatory freight rates. "This freight rate business is the heart of the whole Southern problem," Governor Bibb Graves of Alabama declared. "It explains nearly everything. Poverty. Low wages. Bad housing. We can't move till we get free." In the late thirties freight rates became the subject of a great sectional crusade that enlisted almost universal support in the South and powerful allies in the administration. By a combination of persistent agitation and pressure on several fronts the movement eventually swept on to victory.

In retrospect, however, economists regard regionalized freight rates as only a minor barrier to regional development, and one that gradually would have yielded in any case. In other respects, too, economists have challenged the analyses of the thirties. In a 1964 essay Clarence H. Danhof criticized the concept of the colonial economy as touched with paranoia. "The colonial-imperialistic thesis of conspiracy," he wrote, "must be considered an unfortunate episode—a resurgence of crude sectionalism—that diverted the attention of some of the South's ablest men from constructive approaches to the region's problems."

Viewing the scene from the vantage point of the mid-sixties, he found untenable many of the attitudes associated with that school of thought. The tariff, Danhof noted, ceased to be a regional issue with lessened southern dependence upon foreign agricultural markets. The old complaints about stabilization and monopoly have less validity in an economy growing nationally, with a high degree of expansion directed to the South. And absentee-ownership of branch plants in a highly organized national economy has become the rule rather than the exception everywhere. Branch plants in the South have contributed capital, modern technology, and managerial skills; they have developed incomes that otherwise would not be available, and in places have brought a healthy diversification in their train. To some extent the old argument about southern wage differentials is still alive. Population pressure continues, but the region has absorbed federal minimum standards without damaging consequences, and cheap unskilled labor is losing its power as a magnet for industry. The sectors of most promising growth potential are those enticed by labor skills, attractive communities, and growing markets. In recent decades, the South has moved into secondary and tertiary economic activities on a large scale; the greatest sources of income growth have been in tertiary occupations rather than manufacturing: in government, trade, and services.

The effect of economic activity since the thirties, then, has rendered archaic many of the concerns of that decade. Some would deny that they ever reflected a valid analysis. But economists in recent years have provided a new frame of reference. They have given us the magic phrase, "economic development," which puts the thirties in a historical perspective that suggests a transitional stage of economic growth and economic thought. Much of the colonial revolt against the imperial North echoed old themes of Jeffersonian agrarianism and populism, but with a significant difference: the rebellious southerners did not look back to a rural Arcadia but forward to an industrial South. They geared the force of sectional feeling to a different theme, the theme of economic growth. Few of them were professional economists. They were sociologists, historians, publicists, and politicians. But to a significant degree they anticipated themes later developed by economists.

The economic report of 1938, Arthur Goldschmidt has noted, "covered to a remarkable extent the same range of problems discussed by experts currently reviewing similar underdeveloped segments of the world for the United Nations, the World Bank or U. S. foreign-aid agencies." The report afforded a perspective broader than the traditional New South theme of industry-hunting, of enticing vagrant garment factories. It presented economic development in terms of a broad range of problems: agricultural readjustment, governmental policies, education, resource development, human welfare, purchasing power. It was a long step toward the insight more explicitly developed by William T. Nicholls in his *Southern Tradition and Regional Progress*, a step toward the recognition that economic development is related to the entire social and cultural milieu.

Since World War II economists have come to dominate the study of regional development that was originally the domain of the sociologists. The organization of the National Planning Association's Committee of the South in 1946 marked a turning point. Among other projects, it sponsored the preparation of Hoover and Ratchford's *Economic Resources and Policies of the South* and Glenn McLaughlin and Stefan Robock's *Why Industry Moves South*. Later the Inter-University Committee for Economic Research on the South sponsored another body of publications in the field, including the *Essays in Economic Development in the South*.

The economists have explored new themes that I have neither the time nor the competence to pursue here. Their most important contribution, perhaps, has been to broaden perspectives on economic development. One of the salient features of the broader landscape they have developed is represented in such phenomena as the Southern Research Institute, the Research Triangle, the Southern Regional Growth Policies Board, and that Tennessee advertisement in the New York *Times*. It suggests that the one area in which conscious effort by states and communities can most surely advance economic growth is in the development of education, labor skills, and scientific research. In the words of Clarence Danhof, "Persistent adherence to the fundamental task of upgrading human capabilities is the region's best guarantee of continued growth."

11

Onward and Upward
with the Rising South

IT MAY SEEM PEEVISH AND UNGRACIOUS TO BEGIN A CELE-
bration of "The Rising South" on a note of paradox and
irony. But one of the occupational hazards of historians
is a weakness for skepticism and a sense of kinship with
the ancient sage who wrote in the book of Ecclesiastes:
"The thing that hath been, it is that which shall be; and
that which is done is that which shall be done: and there
is no new thing under the sun. . . . There is no remembrance of former things; neither shall there be any
remembrance of things that are to come with those that
come after."

The symposium on the South is itself a thing that
hath been and that shall be. For among the imponder-
ables and uncertainties of the changing South there
seems to be one durable constant—somebody will always
be staging a symposium on the changing South. It is one
of the flourishing minor industries of the region, one in
which countless professional southerners have built up
a vested interest. But it has been a cyclical industry,

which fluctuates unpredictably: 1972 was the best year recently, when two major symposia took place within a span of two months, in Tampa and Chapel Hill. The best year of the previous decade was 1965, when the centennial of Appomattox gave rise to a flood of commentaries, including special issues of *Harpers*, *Look*, and *Newsweek*, and a book entitled *The South in Continuity and Change*, issued by Duke University Press. Another flood is no doubt coming with the Revolutionary bicentennial.

If one has a taste for tedium one can trace it back through the musty indexes until the standard title becomes the "New South," that being the subject of a symposium reported in *Review of Reviews* during 1892. With enough perseverance, in fact, one might go on back to those antebellum commercial conventions that kept whooping it up for the rising South. Whether this practice had origins in the colonial period, I cannot say, but one should not be surprised to discover that the French Governor Bienville, before he moved from Mobile to New Orleans back in 1718, held a *pourparler* on "Le Sud changeant."

The themes of these colloquies have been constant for at least a century. The standard topics are economics, race, and politics. Industry is rising, the South is becoming urbanized, all this is having profound effects on racial relations and politics. Another consistent theme has been the Vanishing South, forever moving toward the mainstream of American life but somehow never getting there.

But however clouded the crystal ball may have been, the focus of these confabulations has been clear. The

central theme has been change, and the consciousness
of change has long been one of the established constants
in southern history. "The people of the South," Vann
Woodward wrote in *The Strange Career of Jim Crow*,
"should be the last Americans to expect indefinite continuity of their institutions and social arrangements."
Consider the transformations that have occurred since
Eli Whitney's gin gave rise to the cotton kingdom: the
westward movement of the cotton belt (eventually to
California), the sectional conflict, the rise and fall of the
Confederacy, emancipation, the regime of Reconstruction, replaced in turn by that of the New South, which
faced down challenge from the Populists, then assimi-
lated the progressives and New Dealers. And consider
the changes wrought in the twentieth century by technology, industry, and urbanization. Within three decades we have watched the landmarks topple in rapid
succession: the one-crop agriculture, the one-crop industry, the one-party system, the white primary, the poll
tax, racial segregation—indeed so many foundations of
the old order that we now live in a post-New South
which nobody has yet given a name.

But throughout all the flux of change there have persisted certain constants. Not long ago an example of
one jumped up from the front page of my hometown
newspaper, the Greenville *News-Piedmont* for February
17, 1974. A seductive headline ran across the bottom
of the front page: "S. C. Piedmont Is Becoming the
Energy Capital of the World." In the story that followed
and in a sequel the next day the writer asserted: "The
potential for economic growth in the Piedmont appears
to be unrivaled by any other area in this country and
perhaps the world." The reason for this miracle was that

Duke Power Company was building a nuclear plant near Gaffney and had another over in Oconee County. Visiting the area of the proposed Cherokee Nuclear Station in a "sparsely populated, undeveloped section of the county," the writer found it obvious "that this area of pine thickets and fields of broomstraw, milkweed, and briars could only benefit by the nearness of the giant power plant with its towering plumed stacks." He anticipated a new industrial park and a new residential area. If he had ever heard of ecology or the Club of Rome, if he had ever seen the dark satanic mills of Birmingham or felt the rattling rhythm of a weave-room, he did not let on.

Neither, in all likelihood, did he write from a conscious remembrance of former things, but his articles belong to a venerable tradition of the South. They betray a penchant for the superlative, which caught the eye of a Harvard historian some years ago. In *The Southern South*, a book published in 1910, historian Albert Bushnell Hart quoted a comment by Walter Hines Page on the "oratorical habit of mind" that had afflicted the postwar generation. "Rousing speech," Page had written, "was more to be desired than accuracy of statement. An exaggerated manner and a tendency to sweeping generalizations were the results." Hart then added his own observation: "Another form of this habit of mind is the love of round numbers, a fondness for stating a thing in the largest terms; thus the clever but no-wise distinguished professor of Latin is 'Probably the greatest classical scholar in the United States,' the siege of Vicksburg was 'the most terrific contest in the annals of warfare'; the material progress of the South is 'the most marvelous thing in human history.'"

It's odd how these habits persist. The booster rhetoric in the Greenville *News-Piedmont* might have been lifted, with slight alteration, from one of those articles the *Manufacturers Record* used to run in the 1920s on the glorious future of hydroelectric "Super-Power," the great "region builder." In fact the sound of the booster rhetoric is about as up-to-date as the music of an Elizabethan ballad or the prose of Sir Walter Raleigh exhorting his countrymen to get in on the New World bonanza. A few years ago, in the journal *Louisiana History*, historian Charles P. Roland remarked on this durable infatuation: the South's persistent sense of destiny, the perennial belief that the region is on the verge of economic fulfillment. Roland began with Lyndon Johnson's proposition that the "crescent of the Gulf offers one of the great opportunities of the Western World"; then he flashed back to Thomas Hariot's report from Roanoke Island that "in a short time the planters may . . . enrich themselves and those who trade with them." Then Roland pursued the boosters back to the present, citing along the way, and among others: Hugh Jones, John Lawson, Thomas Jefferson, John C. Calhoun, James H. Hammond, Hinton R. Helper, Henry W. Grady, Francis Dawson, Edwin Mims, Franklin D. Roosevelt, and Walter Prescott Webb. "The South," Roland asserted, "has persistently been the nation's greatest economic enigma —a region of want in the midst of boundless natural riches. It has been, and remains today, a land becoming and not a land become—a garden spot that beckons only to recede like a mirage when approached. It is America's will-o'-the wisp Eden."

One major reason has been the South's fatal affinity for low-wage industries. A few years ago two economists conducted a survey of new plants located in Tennessee between 1955 and 1965. They asked the managers to evaluate the factors that determined their location. The factor most often mentioned and the one assigned the most weight was the low cost and availability of labor. Cheap Anglo-Saxon workers are no longer "offered on the auction block pretty much as their black predecessors were," to quote Broadus Mitchell, at least not so openly. But the Georgia Department of Community Development recently inserted an advertisement in the *Wall Street Journal* which asked: "Is an honest day's work for an honest day's pay an old-fashioned attitude?" The answer was: "Not in Georgia. In our smaller towns, you'll find people who are eager to work. . . . Manpower is one of our State's greatest assets." The words are unimpeachable, but what lies between the lines is something else again.

Of course there is a dilemma for the South in this predicament. Even sweatshops, sad to relate, may give a leg up to displaced field hands. One must learn to crawl before he can walk, and any balanced picture of southern development must show the vistas of opportunity that have opened in the past. Millions of southerners, most often white but sometimes black, have moved up from farm to mill village and town, from tenancy or yeomanry to middle-class affluence. A review of statistics will show that, at least since 1880, industrial development in the region has moved at a faster pace than in the nation at large, and that the gap between North and South continues to narrow.

Per capita income has followed a similar path. Excluding Texas and Oklahoma, which would have made the averages still higher, per capita incomes that were only 69.1 percent of the national average in 1959 had reached 73 percent in 1963, and 80 percent in 1972. The out-migration that has made the South historically a seedbed of population for the rest of the country has been reversed since the mid-1950s. During the 1960s the South had a total net in-migration of nearly 500,000 despite a new loss of nearly 1.5 million blacks. And lately it seems that many blacks are returning.

By the 1950s the region scored its urban breakthrough. By 1960 the population was 58 percent urban and by 1970, it was 64.6 percent urban. And only a small part of the remainder were still farming. In the states of the former Confederacy in 1964, only about 8 percent of the population remained on farms—about 3.8 million southerners. And farming has undergone sweeping changes. "The bizarre incident of the New Deal plow-up in 1933," historian Tom Clark wrote, "closed the ledger on an era of Southern history that began with Eli Whitney." In 1969, the South was growing only about 79 percent of the nation's cotton, and the crop fetched only about 7 percent of the total worth of southern farm products. Poultry and eggs accounted for nearly three times as much, cattle for nearly four times as much, cattle and dairy products combined for nearly five times as much. Green pastures and motels for chickens have become features of the landscape as common as the endless rows of cotton used to be. If the streams still run muddy, it is because of building projects rather than eroded fields.

There are some other gratifying features in the new landscape. Being late to develop, southern industry has escaped the urgent need to converge on power sources and railheads. Electricity, petroleum, and natural gas can go by cable or pipeline, the products can go by truck, and the mills can straggle across the landscape. The idyllic vision of factory-farm living has become reality for many and should prevail widely so long as the petroleum holds out. But nobody who has driven through the Southern Ruhr Valley along the Mississippi between Baton Rouge and New Orleans, and nobody who has fought his way through the shabby strips that lead to southern cities can be unaware of greater pitfalls ahead.

An even more desperate consequence of change is an abomination that keeps away from the sight of comfortable people, like the dark side of the moon: the multitudes left stranded in the backwaters of economic development. After Senator Ernest M. Hollings, Jr., had toured some of the rural slums down home in South Carolina, he admitted to a Senate committee that as governor he had supported "the public policy of covering up the problem of hunger" in the interest of attracting new industry and creating jobs. "I know the need for jobs," he said, "but what I am talking about here . . . is downright hunger. The people I saw couldn't possibly work."

Perhaps better planning could help bring about more rational development, but it affords no panacea. Even so enlightened an enterprise as the Tennessee Valley Authority has become a voracious consumer of strip-mined coal and has come under attack for other sins against the public. It is an old experience that public regulatory agencies tend to fall under the sway of those they are supposed to restrain. Vested interests and real-estate promoters repeatedly bend planning boards to their own purposes.

Years ago the New Deal offered funds to encourage

the development of planning agencies. By 1935 all the southern governors had appointed planning boards, and by 1938 all the boards had statutory authority. Their purpose, as the Arkansas planners put it in 1936, was the "common sense principle of directing the future physical development of a state in accordance with a comprehensive long-term coordinated plan" which would "take into account many social and economic considerations." In 1940 the governors of seven states set up a Southeastern Regional Planning Commission to correlate the programs.

But planning took a low priority. The state boards had scarcely moved beyond general surveys when the pressure for payrolls caused their transformation into development boards. So agencies that started with some promise of broad-gauged social planning ended as agencies to lure the vagrant factories. Maybe the movement came forty years too soon and maybe new payrolls were what a backward region most desperately needed, but the momentum for planning was lost.

The ironies of history that overtake the best-laid schemes have unfolded once again in the movements for black liberation. The changes in racial relations, of course, have produced the most vivid human drama in the recent South, and the most emotionally wrenching. Surely, one may think, these things must be unparalleled in the southern past: the dramatic confrontations, the new legal rights attained by black southerners, the sudden collapse of massive resistance, and the turn to more subtle forms of white resistance.

In 1974 the South's leading segregationist won renomination for governor after a campaign in which he openly courted the black vote. In 1963 he had cast down the gauntlet and proclaimed: "Segregation now, segregation forever." Forever, it turned out, lasted about ten years. But as Harold Wilson has said, one week is a long time in politics.

Such a sudden collapse of resistance had occurred before, in the far more wrenching drama of emancipation. And according to historian Clement Eaton, "[O]ne of the most striking aspects of the Southern mood after Appomattox was the widespread expression of approval, even relief, that slavery had been abolished. Ex-Governor Henry A. Wise of Virginia, for example, declared in an open address on June 17, 1873, before Roanoke College that slavery was the worst curse that had ever rested on the Southern people and that it had been a great incubus on Southern development."

The threat to segregation, like the threat to slavery, however, brought forth a stubborn defense. The White Citizens' Councils, for example, had their counterparts in the vigilance committees of the Old South. The effort to justify segregation revived many points of the proslavery argument, in altered form. The doctrine of interposition revived, or sought to revive, an old doctrine of states' rights. But the resistance to civil rights proved to be a pale replica of the resistance to abolition, perhaps because southerners recognized the truth of what Governor Earl Long told the Louisiana legislature: They had to realize that the Feds have got the A-bomb now.

Historians always protest reluctance to don the robes of prophecy, but they protest too much, because they are always doing it under the guise of showing trends from the past. In a paper first delivered in 1955 and published as Chapter 4 of this volume under the title,

"The Central Theme Revisited," I suggested that the spell cast by the old southern credo on race and the widespread assumption that it was the central explanation of southern character obscured the equally fundamental role of its antithesis, the American creed of equality, which a white southerner defined in 1776. "Thus criticism of southern racial practice has repeatedly generated temporary intransigence, but in the long run and more significantly it has also compelled self-justification and a slow but steady adjustment by white Southerners in the direction of the American faith in equality of opportunity and rights." This is not, of course, to ignore other factors—religious, social, ideological, economic, and political—that have contributed to the white adjustment.

Black reactions have evinced historical parallels, too. The Montgomery bus boycott, which began a long sequence of dramatic confrontations, had its counterpart in the streetcar boycotts that protested the imposition of Jim Crow requirements at the turn of the century. The new legal rights won in court decisions and in the climactic Civil Rights and Voting Rights Acts had their counterparts and much of their basis in the Reconstruction Amendments, which lay dormant through the later reaction but came back to life in the twentieth century.

The millennial hopes and the Biblical rhetoric of Martin Luther King's civil rights movement had their parallels in the crusade against slavery. Both maintained a high level of moral exaltation, which could not last indefinitely, but both, in fact, achieved their objectives of fixing certain principles in the law of the land, if not yet in the practice of the land. Each of the former institutions left its shadow to haunt posterity. Slavery, in the guise of peonage, still lingers in the boondocks. Segregation, in the guise of the private academy, flourishes today. Emancipation freed the slaves, but failed to deliver forty acres and a mule. Civil rights opened up the restaurants, but failed to provide for the check.

In the aftermath of slavery, tenancy and the failure of the Freedmen's Savings Bank taught paradoxical lessons in the improvidence of thrift and the value of living for the day—before somebody took it away from you. In the aftermath of segregation, the urban ghetto taught lessons in brigandage and looting—because nobody was going to give it to you. At least the latter expressed a revolution of rising expectations. The Civil Rights Act of 1964, moreover, set up a ban on discrimination in jobs and education which, in turn, has brought on programs to provide special restitution for the deprivations of the past. However ill-designed they may be in some instances, these things go well beyond the transient relief offered by the Freedmen's Bureau after the Civil War. Their legality, however, remains an unsettled question. The Supreme Court has so far dodged a resolution of the issue.

Disappointment with the gains achieved by emancipation and civil rights left a heritage of disillusionment, and the discontent in each case gave rise to movements that turned inward upon the black community: first Booker T. Washington and his policy of accommodation, vocational studies, and self-help; more recently black power and a policy of defiance, black studies, and separatism. More than one white has confessed puzzlement at the ramifications of the black power movement, and has asked in unconscious echo of Sigmund Freud's question about women: "What do they want?" Surely nobody, white or black, has the definitive answer, but historical perspectives suggest that black power gives a new name and a new manifestation to what used to be called Negro nationalism, an undercurrent that has always moved in the black community and that has surfaced most conspicuously in two mass movements of the twentieth century: Marcus Garvey's back-to-Africa crusade of the 1920s and the separatist movement to which Stokely Carmichael gave the name "black power" in 1966.

The movements shared a common slogan, "Black is beautiful," and a common fear that integration would destroy a black identity. Both have had their chief seat in the urban North and both have had among their most conspicuous leaders natives of the West Indies where a continuing sense of identification with black Africa has nourished the social myth of *négritude*.

At some point, however, the parallels begin to break down, and the connecting lines begin to cross over one another. Sometimes black power looks like Booker T. Washington warmed over and spiced up with a dash of Karl Marx—or is it Marcus Garvey warmed over and spiced up with a dash of Marshall McLuhan? Or more appropriately, perhaps, is it two strange mixtures of Washington the accommodationist and his old adversary, W. E. B. Du Bois, the egalitarian. The formula for black power seems to mix equal portions of Washington's self-help and Du Bois's proud defiance, while the recipe for integration seems to mix equal portions of Washington's restraint and Du Bois's quest for equal rights.

In retrospect, however, Washington and Du Bois emerge less as the champions of incompatible philosophies than as the complementary leaders of a common struggle carried on at two levels, the one laying a foundation for the growing success of the other's approach. Can it be that eventually the integrationists and separatists of the present will emerge as the complementary poles of a similar dialectic, moving toward a synthesis already dimly seen: an ongoing ethnic identity within an integrated society, so that being an Afro-American will be something like being an Irish-American or a Polish-American—or, for that matter, a southern-white-American? Such an outcome might combine the best of both worlds, achieving cultural and psychological fulfillment without discarding political and economic goals.

It has become common now to speak of a first and second Reconstruction, the two occurring about a century apart. They were alike in achieving certain goals, and alike in the disillusionment and the reactions that followed. They seem to have been different in their political effects, however: one destroyed the chances for a two-party system, the other seems to have improved the chances. Yet, although the tides move in a different direction now, the politics of the South have come back into a state of flux something like that which existed in the lost years before the triumph of Jim Crow and the Solid South at the turn of the century. Southern politics is open once again to the strategies of coalition that Presidents Hayes, Garfield, Arthur, and Harrison tried to exploit, but with little success.

After Reconstruction every southern strategy failed the Republicans: first the effort by Hayes to enlist southern conservatives, then the effort by Garfield and

Arthur to enlist southern insurgents. The stigma of Reconstruction, however unfair it may have been, was too much to overcome and the party ceased to offer effective opposition except in parts of the upper South.

Ever since the 1920s, however, new conditions have caused repeated disruptions of southern Democracy: the clash between metropolitan and rural values in 1924 and 1928, sectional tensions aroused by the New Deal, the shift of black voters to the Democratic party, and the rise of the civil rights movement. The Dixiecrat rebellion marked the end of the Solid South in the electoral college.

With the election of Dwight D. Eisenhower in 1952 Hayes's strategy at last succeeded. The beneficiary of a kind of "conservative chic" in the burgeoning suburbs, Eisenhower also garnered a sizable black vote and carried several states of the outer South. Nixon's vote in 1960, although smaller, followed the same pattern, but Goldwater in 1964 and Nixon in 1968 and after gave the southern strategy a new twist.

Abandoning the black vote (once traditionally Republican) just as it was on the rise, and combining Hayes's appeal to conservatives with Arthur's appeal to insurgents, Goldwater and Nixon wooed simultaneously the silk-stockinged suburbanites and the rebellious segregationists. Both encountered trouble—Goldwater in suburbia and Nixon in Wallace country—and whether such an unlikely coalition can long endure remains to be seen, and at what cost to the party of the Great Emancipator.

Democrats, however, had been able to hold plebeian and patrician in the same party for many years. The South, "more than any other part of the country, retains the idea of the Gentry versus the Lower Classes," Sinclair Lewis wrote in 1929 after visiting the scene of the strike at Marion, North Carolina. But he added: "It doesn't take much to feel that you are in the Gentry. Owning a small grocery ... will do it." In the New South, as in the Old, one did not have to share the power of the elite in order to share the mystique.

One of the neglected areas of recent southern history, George Mowry has said, is this persistent "elite and its relationship to the area's politicians." Even such an expert on southern politics as V. O. Key, Jr., Mowry noted, had to be equivocal on the subject for want of clear knowledge. The result of the existing system, however, was more certain—"a social and economic structure in which the gulf between the rich and the poor has been extraordinarily wide." The record, Mowry said, "is written in beating back the twin threats of liberal or progressive state governments and of labor unions, in maintaining the wage differentials between classes within the South, and by comparison to those existing elsewhere in the nation, and in holding to a minimum federal intervention in either the industrial or the racial question." At least for a long time. And the two questions were connected: "Sustained racial passions meant one-party government, one-party government meant upper-class control, and hence antiunion government, Q. E. D.: a certain level of racial animosity worked to the benefit of the owning classes."

Nevertheless, within the last twenty years Republicans have created a durable opposition in the South for the first time since the heyday of the Whigs in the 1840s. With the rise of a two-party system, therefore, southern politics seems headed toward a more schematic arrangement than in the past, with an electorate, now unburdened of the old restrictions, drawn into greater participation by party competition. The new situation has opened southern politics to a wider range of possibilities.

The outcome depends largely upon the directions taken by those groups that have felt most aggrieved in the recent past: the five million or so Wallace voters and the five million or so black voters. The variant possibilities are highlighted by the recent experience of the two cities that elected black members of Congress in 1972. In Houston a coalition of blacks with plebeian whites has developed while in Atlanta black politicians have gained support among the white elite. Either way, coalition politics enhances the chances for reconciliation between the races.

Accounts of Maynard Jackson's inauguration as mayor of Atlanta almost persuade one that there is a new thing under the sun after all. At least we have come a long way from those malicious cartoons of black Sambo in the Reconstruction legislature with a cigar in his face and his feet on the desk. The installation of Atlanta's black mayor may have been the most elegant political event ever staged in the South. The mayor's aunt, Mattiwilda Dobbs, presented spirituals and an operatic aria and the Atlanta Symphony under Robert Shaw presented the choral finale of Beethoven's Ninth Symphony which sets to music the triumphant words of Schiller's "Ode to Joy": *Alle Menschen werden Brüder.* All mankind shall be brothers. And to go from the sublime to the ridiculous, as it were, one might tune in the latest country-music sensation, Tanya Tucker, singing "I Believe the South Is Gonna Rise Again": "A brand new breeze is blowin' cross the southland," it goes, "And I see a brand new kind of brotherhood."

Wide vistas of opportunity beckon at last, and if a leadership can emerge with the genius to seize the day, the South can exploit a chance that comes to few generations. Reconciliation is not out of reach, the land remains relatively unspoiled, the political system is more open and unrestricted than ever before. It may be something of a cliche now, but it is also a self-evident truth, that a region so late in developing has a chance to learn from the mistakes of others.

What Lewis Mumford said about a visit to North Carolina twenty-five years ago remains almost as true today as it was then: "Most of the measures that must be taken in the South may be of a positive rather than a remedial nature; they are matters of preserving a balance that still exists, rather than of re-establishing a balance that has been almost utterly destroyed."

But before this begins to sound like Henry Grady warmed over and spiced up with a dash of Pollyanna, let us not forget that if experience is any guide, the South will blow it. We will have to make the same mistakes all over again, and we will achieve the urban blight, the crowding, the traffic jams, the slums, the ghettos, the pollution, the frenzy, and all the other ills that modern man is heir to. We are already well on the way.

Index

Williams, Tennessee, 28
Williams, William Appleman, 12
Wilson, Woodrow, 137, 144–45, 147
Wise, Henry A., 233
Wolfe, Thomas, 38, 147
Wolfe, Tom, 9–10
Woodward, C. Vann: and *American Counterpoint*, 16; and "The Popu-
list Heritage and the Intellectual," 169; and *Origins of the New South*, 217–18; and *The Strange Career of Jim Crow*, 226; mentioned, 12, 15, 21, 34, 37, 42, 63, 72, 136, 144

Yeoman farmers, 27, 33
Young, Owen D., 105